Sales Insights from a
Herman Miller Watercarrier

Sales Insights from a Herman Miller Watercarrier

Bryan Dozeman

iUniverse, Inc.
New York Lincoln Shanghai

Sales Insights from a Herman Miller Watercarrier

iUniverse books may be ordered through booksellers or by contacting:

iUniverse
2021 Pine Lake Road, Suite 100
Lincoln, NE 68512
www.iuniverse.com
1-800-Authors (1-800-288-4677)

ISBN-13: 978-0-595-37542-4 (pbk)
ISBN-13: 978-0-595-81936-2 (ebk)
ISBN-10: 0-595-37542-1 (pbk)
ISBN-10: 0-595-81936-2 (ebk)

Printed in the United States of America

To my wonderful wife, Pat, who for the past thirty-four years has constantly reminded me to "write it down!"

Contents

Acknowledgments

I never thought that I would write a book. After many years of representing Herman Miller, Inc., however, and working with our dealerships and serving our customers, I found myself with stories and insights that could help others in the sales profession.

So how do I take my sales experience and transform it into a written document?

Two words: Clark Malcolm. Creating this book with Clark, who has written and edited many things for Herman Miller, has been a wonderful learning experience. I appreciate his expertise, his guidance, his candor, and his friendship.

I also owe a great deal to Patricia Dozeman, my wife and my friend. Pat not only encouraged me to write down these stories and experiences but also took the time to critique and review every word.

Many thanks also to all of the people at Herman Miller who have enriched my life by allowing me to learn while being part of this wonderful culture.

I want to thank Herman Miller's dealers who taught me the art of salesmanship and the benefits of teamwork.

And I would like to give a special thank-you to all of my customers. They made my career possible, influenced my development as a salesperson, and taught me how to identify and solve problems.

Foreword

I love sales. I have been in sales for more than thirty-five years. To me, sales is the most interesting, challenging, and rewarding vocation anyone could ever choose. After all, in most businesses nothing happens until somebody makes a sale. No other career gives you a greater high when you win or one terrible low when you lose. Sales is an all-or-nothing game.

I am most fortunate that my entire sales career has evolved around a great organization, Herman Miller, Inc., a global provider of office furniture and services that helps create great places to work, live, heal, and learn. This world-renowned organization is known for quality, innovation, and respect for its employees. As a mark of thanks and respect, Herman Miller names all employees with twenty years of service Watercarriers.

Max De Pree, the former chairman who began this honor, described his idea in his well-known book *Leadership Jazz*. Here is the way Herman Miller talks about Watercarriers:

> Water is at once a necessity for life and an enduring symbol of sustenance and rejuvenation. Tribal watercarriers thus hold a special position, one of importance and responsibility. They bear and supply one of the body's and the spirit's more basic elements.
> Corporations, like tribes, have watercarriers, people who preserve and exemplify for the group the essential elements of continuity and commitment. Corporations, no less than tribes, honor and esteem their watercarriers.

As a Herman Miller Watercarrier, I want to take this opportunity to pass along to others my experience and lessons learned as a salesperson.

I first thought about sales in my high school English class. My teacher thought it would be fascinating to be a salesperson. How challenging it would be to walk into a sales situation armed with nothing but your wit, knowledge, and ability to communicate. If you were good enough, you would walk out with an order. That sounded exciting, especially to somebody who didn't like to read or write.

How do salespeople become good at what they do? I don't remember any textbook that said it all. I certainly learned by making mistakes. (Fortunately, most of my colleagues today are too young to remember them.) Above all, I learned by watching and listening to the masters, the proven sales professionals. These unique individuals were problem solvers, and, as a result of their talent and hard work, they booked lots of orders. These were people who knew how to prospect for new accounts. People who knew how to handle objections. Professionals who would give dynamic presentations and turn objections into positive buying signals. I took their techniques and their styles and adopted them into my own work habits.

Before now, I've seldom had the opportunity to pass along the ideas and practices other people have given me over the years. Now is the time. This little book is a series of ideas, phrases, suggestions, warnings, gimmicks, attitudes, stories, and thoughts. They are not formulas. Some of the greatest salespeople in the office-furnishings industry today have shown me that these lessons work in the field. I somehow think that the people from whom I learned so much will not mind my passing these lessons on to others. Salespeople take a lot of pleasure in the success of others. Whether you consider yourself a salesperson or not, remember that we are all working to communicate, inform, and persuade. Whether we admit it or not, we all have something to sell. I hope this book helps you to become a better presenter, communicator, and sales professional.

1

Get Ready

Whether you are planning for a weekend retreat or a 'round-the-world cruise, you need to prepare yourself for the adventure. The same holds true if you are going to give the most important sales presentation of your career, or if you are simply trying to convince your spouse where to keep the checkbook. When you are preparing for a meeting, discussion, or presentation, understanding both your audience and yourself can make the difference between success and failure.

Take Out the Garbage

Many books have been written on the sales process. I think I can reduce the entire bookshelf to one simple phrase: "Get the garbage off your client's plate." Think about it: Today everybody has a lot on his or her plate. There is the stress of completing the job on time with less support, and doing it better and faster. Everyone is taking on more assignments. All our plates are full to overflowing.

Whether you are getting a new mortgage or the car repaired, you want somebody to do it right the first time, as fast as possible, and at a fair price. You are too busy to go back two or three times. Our clients feel the same way. Whatever product or service you provide, chances are it is not the only product or service that a client is managing. Just like you, a client is dealing with far too many things simultaneously.

Now comes the next step: figuring out how big your clients' plates are and what the garbage is. Once you can figure out what is going on in their lives, what is on their plates, and what keeps them awake at night, then you have a start on how to help them. You need to know your clients better than they know themselves. To get this information, you are going to have to do some digging, talk to people, look on the Internet, and find out what their companies are all about. Who is their competition? How do they differentiate themselves from their competition? Where is their growth? What are their issues? Once you begin to identify their problems, you can begin to develop solutions for them. After all, you are selling solutions, not things. Your client invests in solutions, not objects.

Here is an exercise I use to simplify my client's life. I list five things that keep her up at night. If I cannot come up with a list, I do some digging and get to know my client better. Then I make a list of products or services and show how they can help solve my client's problems. Remember, if you cannot bring value to her or help her in her day-to-day activities, ask yourself, "Why does she need me?"

If you are in touch with your clients, understand their problems, and can reduce the piles of garbage on their plates, you can simplify their lives. If you can make their problems go away, you can speed up their process and make them look good. If you provide them with a valid solution to their problems, they will do everything in their power to give you as much future business as possible. Sales is simple, right? Right.

Don't *Add* to the Garbage

Believe it or not, sometimes we are the ones who actually put *more* garbage on a client's plate.

Have you ever responded to a bid? Did you think that just maybe the more information you put into your response, the more likely it will be that the client will select you? You might be right if bids were awarded based on the weight of the proposal. When you deliver an overweight proposal, you have actually added to your client's work load. *You have put another pile of garbage on your client's plate!* They now have more to read, more to digest, and more to filter through to arrive at a decision.

When you ask a question, do you want a straight, short answer or a thirty-minute lecture on the topic? Our clients are looking for a complete, to-the-point response to their questions. Give them what they are asking for and no more. Many orders have been lost after the sale because of the salesperson's desire to keep talking. When you get the "OK, we'll go with your proposal," say thank you and leave.

It is much the same with a bid. Supply your clients with the information they request. If they want additional information, they will ask. This will lead to additional conversation and possibly negotiations. I have never cashed a commission check that resulted from a thick three-ring binder filled with unnecessary brochures or custom artwork.

Here is a story about a salesperson who knew how to avoid adding garbage. I had the privilege of working with a young creative salesperson by the name of Bret Abbott in Minneapolis. Bret was working with a real estate organization with branch offices in multiple locations. He put together a simplified way for all the branch offices to order seating. The client could use one order sheet by simply filling in the PO number and ship-to address and selecting the different quantity of chairs. The client loved the idea, and all that was needed was to determine the fabric color. At the final meeting, the client asked, "Bret, what do you think we should use for the fabric color?" Bret had been thinking about that, and after looking at the organizational color schemes, he thought a simple, dark color would be the most appropriate.

At this point, Bret opened his briefcase and took out one black hopsack fabric swatch and placed it in front of the client. She held the swatch, looked at it, and said, "I'm afraid this might be a little too dark." Bret responded, "I thought that might be the case, so I took the liberty of bringing an alternative color swatch." She took the dark gray sample Bret proffered and said, "This is perfect." The second sample became the standard for the entire organization.

I was amazed by Bret's foresight. He was so disciplined in providing the client with only two samples. I knew in my heart that if I were suggesting a fabric, I probably would have produced three or four rings of swatches. I might even have brought along the entire fabric program with some eight hundred selections. I know better these days.

What Can You Influence?

A salesperson named David Rose once shared with our sales force an interesting Steven Covey concept. David talked about the "sphere of influence," the area of life that we think we can control. To make his point, David drew a large bull's-eye on the board with its concentric circles. David pointed out that we think our sphere of influence is usually much larger than it really is. Once we take a close look at this sphere, we begin to realize that we have little or no control over the outer layers. It really is not until you get to the center of those circles, toward the bull's-eye, that you realize you might have some actual impact or influence.

Dealing with a client, your company, your family, and even yourself, you can really influence only certain things. Focus on the items that you can control, and do not waste your time and energy getting frustrated or angry about those you cannot control. When working with a client, be realistic as to just what it is you can or cannot influence regarding their decision-making process. Identify the areas where you can make a difference, and concentrate on them.

Here is an exercise for you to explore your sphere of influence. Draw a series of concentric circles. Beginning with the center, identify those things over which you have total control. Then work outward, listing things that you have little or no influence over. This can be a humbling experience.

Uptight?

Anger is a secondary emotion. People are not just angry. They are angry because of something—frustration, fear, or emotional pain. It is difficult to succeed in sales if you are angry. Likewise, it is difficult to work with a client who is angry.

When I feel myself getting angry, I stop and ask myself, "Why am I angry?" Am I trying to manage things outside of my sphere of influence? Am I frustrated because my company is not supporting me, or my client doesn't seem to understand what I am saying? Am I frustrated because my team members are not contributing to my sales process? Am I annoyed simply because somebody cut me off on the highway?

Of course the big question is, "Can I do anything about it?" If there is something I can do about it, I try to do it! The sooner, the better. If not, I accept it and get on with things. I like to think that I refuse to let something beyond my control ruin my day—or a sale. But sometimes, I just get angry.

Another reason for anger is fear. We are all afraid of something. Have you ever been afraid of losing an order, or not making quota, or not giving your best presentation? These fears can develop into anger, and we begin to blame others. Preparation is the best defense against fear. Take enough time to prepare for the presentation, get the information you need, communicate with your teammates, and stay connected with your client.

Sometimes I find myself getting angry because I believe that someone does not like or respect me. It could be a family member, a friend, a colleague, or a client. I try to think about the relationship, and if something is not right, I go and talk with the person and get at the truth. Sometimes I need to ask, "Have I done something to affect our relationship?"

Anger is not a good thing, especially for salespeople. It is really difficult to have a successful sales call when you are angry. A sales call is a major performance, one that you must be up for each time you walk into your client's office. You need to have a truly positive attitude. You need to radiate success and self-assuredness. You need to realize that your goal for this meeting is simply to make your client as successful as possible. Being angry drains your energy and dilutes the concentration you need to accomplish your goals.

I am big on making lists. I make a list of those things that have made me angry. Are they because of frustration, fear, or hurt feelings? Then I look at each one on my list and decide if I have any influence over the causes. Sometimes I have to admit to myself that even the best salespeople in the world can't change some things.

Who's Mad Now?

If your client is angry, you are going to have to disarm that anger before you can have a positive sales call. A great salesman by the name of Ken Duthler once told me about a very interesting process he used with people who seemed upset or angry. When somebody is angry, even an adult with considerable authority or power, he or she tends to act like a child who will throw a tantrum, pout, or just clam up. They want someone to acknowledge that they are angry. So often, we try to ignore that anger and hope that it goes away, only to find that the tantrums, the pouting, or the facial expressions get worse.

Ken's approach is quite simple. If you feel that somebody is angry, simply acknowledge it by saying, "I can see you're really upset." Watch what happens. Suddenly, the need to prove that they are angry goes away. In some cases, the person won't be sure what to do next. They might just say, "Yes, I am." They might tell you why they are upset, which becomes a great opportunity to begin some dialogue. You can now begin to talk with them and see if there is anything that you could do to help. The point is, you need to know how to deal with anger if you want a successful sales call. We all miss major sales opportunities because either we do not have a clear and positive attitude going in, or our client is not in the mind-set to interact with us.

Love It as Much as They Do

I have always been proud to work for Herman Miller. Most Herman Miller employees are. This sense of pride should be handed down from top management. For salespeople, especially, a sense of pride in our companies translates directly into good performance. It shapes our relationships with clients and colleagues. Sooner or later, our clients pick up something of a sense of pride in our company, too.

Years ago, I got a call from a client. He was unhappy with some of the product that he had purchased from us. Apparently in shipment, one of the fabric wall tiles had been slightly damaged. I went over to visit this client to find out just how bad the damage was and what it would take to fix it. When I saw the tile with the minimally damaged corner, I realized that putting it in a different location could easily hide the damage, and no one would notice the flaw.

But then the client told me the following story. "When I was in law school, I promised myself that when I was successful, I would have a Herman Miller office. After years of working to get my degree and building my practice, I ordered a Herman Miller office. But this is not Herman Miller quality." He took greater pride in my product and in my company than I did! Was I willing to accept less? No way! I believe it is the responsibility of every salesperson to make sure that his or her clients get the results they anticipate—or even *better* than they expect. We replaced the tile, and the client got the Herman Miller office he truly deserved. I got a valuable lesson.

Less Is Better

The founder of Herman Miller, Inc., Mr. D. J. De Pree, once said, "Trim is only used to cover mistakes." I have often thought about that when looking at products we all see every day. We often see trim used to substitute for quality in cars, houses, and a million other items. The more trim we see, the more mistakes there probably are. The purer the design, and the better the workmanship, the less need for trim.

I often ask myself, "How much trim do I use in my life?"

I Would've Already Done It

We have all been taught that asking questions of clients, finding out their needs, and applying the right solutions are absolutely crucial. This may be true for the early days of building a client relationship, but other things become equally important after you have established a long-term relationship.

I had an opportunity to call on a major automotive manufacturer, which unfortunately was not already one of our clients. I managed to develop a good relationship with a number of key people at this organization. One individual, whom we will call Ed, was responsible for corporate facilities. He told me a story about their current and long-time supplier, my competitor. During a routine meeting, the representative of this supplier met with Ed and used the typical phrase, "What can we do for you?" Ed, who had met with this representative many times, said, "Do for me? What can you do for me? You position yourself and your organization as experts in the industry. You have been calling on us for many years. By now you should have a very good understanding of our needs and your capabilities. You should be telling me about what services and products I need, rather than asking me what needs to be done. If I knew what I needed, I would've already had it done."

If you are constantly waiting for a long-time client to tell you what he or she needs, chances are somebody else will soon be filling that client's needs.

Leverage

One of the all-time great designers at Herman Miller was Charles Eames. In a discussion regarding his designs and how he made decisions about them, he reportedly said, "If you solve the problem of one person, you have solved the problem of many."

I know a creative young man, Ed Kruschka, who was frustrated by the problem of having to write out a rent payment check every month. This was his only expense not set up for automatic payment. He wondered why he had to send in his rent check every month in a world with all this technology. So he went out and developed a business that would allow renters to have their rent automatically deducted from their bank accounts. And so another entrepreneur was born.

When trying to solve the problems of your client, remember that when you have solved one client's problem, you have probably solved many clients' problems.

2

Get Help

Any adventure is more difficult when you find yourself in uncharted territories and you have to go it alone. That's why we use guides who have been there before and whose experience ensures our survival. In the business world, your guides can be business associates, coworkers, or managers. A strong management team supporting your goals and coworkers on whom you can rely make a big difference in helping you obtain your objectives. Evaluate and select your resources, but remember: some guides are better than others.

Two Ways? Her Way!

One of the most professional and conscientious individuals I have ever had the opportunity and privilege to work with is a young lady by the name of Dawn Mellberg. Dawn is responsible for the customer service activities as they relate to my key accounts. When I first started working with Dawn on a major project, a situation developed that could have resulted in a missed shipping date. I remember calling Dawn and suggesting that I start making phone calls to our top management to pull out all the stops and expedite this important order.

Dawn and I had been working together for only a short period of time. I really did not know her very well, but she already had a pretty good understanding of how I work. After my suggested call to action, she made this comment: "Well, Bryan, there are two ways we can handle this situation. One is, you can make the calls to all the people you know, get as many different groups involved as possible, and see what happens. Or two, you can just let me do my job, and I will take care of it." Based on her logic, experience, and tone of voice, I decided that it made a lot of sense to go with the second option. It was definitely the right choice. She's the one who knows how to get things done and proved that by getting the product shipped on time.

Some of you may remember the famous words of the Detroit Tiger Manager Sparky Anderson who once said, "If they want to win, let them." When you work with a talented person like Dawn, and she wants to do her job, let her!

Play to Win

I worked for a manager named Carol Austin. At one of our sales meetings, she came up with a rather interesting phrase that made me stop and think. The phrase was "Play to win." I began to think that many times in our lives we simply go through the motions and are not really trying to accomplish anything. Of course, there are times when "playing to play" is perfectly all right. But in our professional lives, especially in sales, if you do not play to win, you need to ask yourself, "Why play at all?"

When you are going after a particular project, and you are not committed to accomplishing your goal—if you are not playing to win—don't play. Do not waste your time and energy—and the time and energy of your team. To win, you need to be committed. We all remember the story of the pig and the chicken getting ready for breakfast. The chicken was going to provide the egg; the chicken was *involved*. But the pig was providing the bacon, and he was *committed*. If you are truly committed to sales, you need to apply all of your resources.

There is one exception: If you are 100 percent confident that there is no possible way for you to win a particular bid proposal, why not bid it at full list price? Think of the fun you will have when your competition realizes just how much money they left on the table and have to report back to their management. And maybe the client will be so taken aback by the difference between your bid and that of your competition that they just might want to meet with you to investigate why your bid was so much higher. This could be a great time to discuss how your solutions truly meet their needs.

Carol also made many interesting comments regarding teamwork. During a strategy session, a number of people were all competing to take the lead role in the same account and were causing a lot of confusion and wasting time. Having heard and seen enough of the jockeying, Carol said, "You guys have to stay in your lane." When you are putting together a complex sales strategy, people will have different roles to play. You need to play your role. You need to stay in your lane. Collisions hurt everyone.

Both/And

During a management seminar, an instructor once talked about responsibility and authority. At first, I thought the two words were almost interchangeable. But as the presenter went into greater detail, I realized the difference. Some of us have been given authority. We are in charge, we have the title, and we set the pace. On the other hand, a lot of us have been given responsibility for completing a specific task. What happens when you have one without the other? It is an interesting dilemma. With authority and no responsibility, we are tempted to take credit and no blame. If we have responsibility and no authority, we often find ourselves unable to summon the resources we need to fulfill our responsibilities. If you want authority, you should also be willing to accept responsibility. If you are given responsibility, you should also be given authority. These two words may be different, but the concepts they represent should never be separated.

Want to Play Office?

We are all guilty of playing office at times, filling an hour or even a day with meaningless activity, but some people can make a career out of it. They tend to spend the majority of their time telling everyone just how busy they are and how difficult their current assignment is. I heard a manager respond to a complaining, office-playing employee, "Don't tell me about the pain, just show me the baby."

A Leader with Vision

When you study the founding father of the Herman Miller Company, Mr. D. J. De Pree, you can still see today the impact he had on this great company.

I had the privilege of meeting D. J. in my early days at Herman Miller when I was working at the Educational Center as the greeter, tour guide, stagehand, and janitor. The Educational Center is where we held our client seminars.

We had a major library display at the Educational Center. To make the display complete, we filled it with over two thousand books on various topics. One day, D. J. walked into the showroom and asked me if we were losing any of our books. I told him that I thought the shelves were looking a little empty. D. J. smiled and said, "The next time we have a library display, let's stock the shelves with only religious books. A religious person would probably not want to steal them. If someone did steal a book, the best thing he could do is read it."

D. J. was also a great a person when it came to understanding working relationships. In many organizations, you often see friction between the sales and manufacturing organizations. During a company meeting, D. J. said, "You can be the best salesperson in the world, but if you don't have quality products to represent, you have nothing to sell. On the other hand, you could be the best manufacturer in the world and produce the best products, but if you don't have a sales force promoting the products, there would be no reason to make them."

Now They Will Call

Do you ever get frustrated when people do not return your phone calls? Have you ever called the home office repeatedly, only to find that you never get a callback? Try this next time. Leave this message: "Please call me back when you get the time. I've got something that will make you rich and famous." Then hang up. You will be surprised at how quickly your phone will ring.

Orders Down, Reports Up

I have noticed over the years a direct correlation between a downturn in business and an increase of paperwork. During an economic downturn, information is especially important to upper management. They need it before making major decisions relating to the business—downsizing, a hiring freeze, reduced budgets, or even program elimination. So the information that middle management can provide to upper management is very important.

Sometimes, however, managers ask for information that does not seem to have any use. I once asked an individual who was requesting an incredible amount of seemingly unimportant information whether anybody had asked *him* for this information and what he planned to do with it. "No one has asked for it yet, but just in case someday, somebody, does ask for it, I would like to have it ready." This person has too much time and too much filing space.

Being in front of clients is how salespeople *generate* information like forecasts, win/loss reports, business plans, delivery evaluations, and executive summaries. Unfortunately, requests for reports from salespeople always seem to increase during a downtime, precisely at the time that salespeople need to be in front of clients. Information is necessary for the organization to survive, and sales calls are necessary for organizations to grow. Middle managers should protect their sales force's time and request only reports that are absolutely necessary. Salespeople should consider the pressures on their managers and remember that the information they are being asked to provide is crucial to the growth, and even the sur-vival, of their organizations.

Your Assignment, Should You Choose to Accept

Very few heroes work independently. The Lone Ranger had Tonto. The Green Hornet had Kato. Batman had Robin. Salespeople need partners, as well.

One of my all-time favorite television shows was *Mission Impossible*. The show began when Jim was given his assignment. He would go back to his apartment, open his briefcase, and review the photographs and dossiers of various "Mission Impossible" team members. Depending on the assignment, Jim would carefully select his team. Salespeople should do basically the same thing. Once we identify the client situation and map out a sales strategy, we should start to go through our portfolio of resources, carefully selecting those people with qualifications nec-essary to get the job done.

It is a simple process, once you understand your resources and how to apply them. In sales, we know it's all about the numbers. And where do the numbers come from? People and projects. The more projects, the more wins, the more commission dollars. So select your team carefully. The better the team, the more wins, the more commission dollars. The next time you are given an assignment or have an opportunity to call on a new account, develop a plan and then assemble your own Mission Impossible team.

Driving or Riding?

Once I asked a client to describe his company's management. He described them this way: "Have you ever gone to an amusement park and seen the little boats in the small round pond and noticed how the little kids sitting in the boats turn the steering wheels, ring the bells, and go through all the motions as though they're really driving the little boats? In reality they are just going along for the ride. Well, that's my management." He thought his managers were simply going along for the ride. Although they thought that they were making the big decisions and believed that they were in control of their organization's destiny, it was the econ-omy that was just pulling them along. It is a sad image, but it is an accurate pic-ture of the management in many corporations.

There are also many organizations blessed with outstanding management. These organizations have management teams with clearly defined visions and goals and have leaders who make the tough decisions about what is needed to succeed and grow. These people really are guiding their boats; they are not along for the ride. When that's the case, I know they are not just going around in circles.

Perceptions Matter

Like many manufacturing organizations, my company has a group of dedicated salespeople reporting directly to the company. Most of our sales and services, however, are accomplished through a network of authorized dealerships. These generally independently owned companies represent our products as well as other noncompeting, complementary product lines. These organizations have designers, installers, and salespeople to support the sales process, and they provide total customer service. In many cases, there is competition over who owns the account. There sometimes exists confusion regarding the roles of a manufacturer's salesperson and the distributor's salesperson. Who was responsible for the account? Who gets the glory for the sale? How do you work in harmony so as not to be duplicating efforts?

A number of years back, while I was working in the Minneapolis market, a new salesperson joined my sales organization. He was concerned about his role and how he was going to support and work with our distribution. I thought it would be a good idea if this rookie could hear firsthand how a distributor views the manufacturer. So I asked one of the distributor's seasoned salespeople to tell our new salesperson just how the veteran saw the two organizations working together. He proceeded to tell the following story:

> It's a cold winter day, and I go out into the woods hunting for deer. I leave the comfort of my cabin early in the morning and walk through the snow and cold and sometimes freezing rain. I spend hours upon hours stalking the game. Once I locate the game, I wait patiently for the perfect shot. I position my rifle and take careful aim. But I don't pull the trigger. Instead, I call you. You drive to the campsite, walk out to my blind, and squeeze the trigger. Then you get back into your warm car and drive back to your cozy little cabin. I track the deer through the snow. I get to field dress it. Then I get to pull it out of the woods. I load it on my truck and drive it to the butcher shop. I pay the butcher, pick up the processed meat, and take it back to my cabin. I turn on the stove and prepare the meat and cook a fabulous meal. And when everything is ready, I call you again. You come over and we have a fine meal.

Who's Got the Monkey?

Where do you go when you need help with a problem? Do you ever wish that you had a "you" to go to? A sales manager once told me a story about people asking him for help. Whenever one of his salespeople would come into the office and start off a conversation by saying, "We have a problem," the sales manager would immediately imagine a big, ugly, hairy monkey sitting on that person's shoulders. The sales manager knew that sooner or later the monkey was going to try to jump off the salesperson's shoulders onto the desk and then onto *his* shoulders. If the sales manager inherited just one monkey per day from each of his salespeople, it would not take too long before he would be hosting an entire roomful of monkeys.

The sales manager told me how really important it was to listen to the salesperson, share ideas, give suggestions, and make recommendations, but when the salesperson left his office, the monkey needed to leave with the salesperson. So many times we try to handle everything ourselves. In many cases we are the ones responsible, and we need to take charge. In many other situations, we need to ask ourselves, "Is this really my responsibility, or am I just collecting monkeys?"

Don't Set off the Alarm

Over the years I have worked for a lot of great managers. One of the best was Mark Kinsler. Mark had the discipline to withhold any unnecessary information that could distract a salesperson from doing his or her job. It is not as though Mark kept me in the dark; Mark shared only the information I needed to complete my work. On the other hand, I also know of managers who use concern, worry, rumors, and bad news as management tools. Some of these managers exercise their power by telling people just how bad a situation is, how much trouble the corporation is in, or what negative impact some upcoming changes are likely to have. Managers who delight in using this negative management approach feel that they are establishing loyalty among their employees by sharing with them this top-secret, inside negative information. In reality, all they are doing is disrupting the salesperson's focus and keeping him or her from concentrating on the job at hand.

Salespeople sometimes behave in the same way with their clients. In trying to appear important, the keeper of inside information, the salesperson does a disservice to clients by providing them with unnecessary and often negative information. I'm not saying we should ever keep our clients in the dark or avoid bad news about their project. But rumors and gossip have no place in a conversation between a salesperson and client. The relationship is simply too important

Eighteen=Never

Deciphering codes can be an exciting adventure, one that many people find fascinating. After sitting through years of planning meetings regarding goals and objectives, I have discovered a unique code in business that people have been using for quite some time. It is called the Eighteen-Month Code.

How many times have you been in a meeting, and, while reviewing a particular business plan someone interjects the phrase, "We hope to accomplish this in eighteen months," or "It will take approximately eighteen months to achieve this objective"? Take note, because you will probably never hear about that goal or objective again. Eighteen months goes beyond the typical yearly business plan. In many cases, the person with the eighteen-month goal or objective is banking on the fact that after a year, when a new plan is written, no one will go back to the original plan and hold anybody accountable. The next time you are at a meeting and somebody uses the famous eighteen months phrase, remember it is probably code for "nothing will ever happen."

Trained by the Best

It was the early 1970s and I had just moved to Chicago to join our sales team, located in the Merchandise Mart. Back then, we did not really have a formalized training program. To "learn the ropes," as my manager put it, he suggested that I fly up to Minneapolis to spend some time with one of our experienced salespeople. So I booked my flight, flew to Minneapolis, and arrived about 9:45 AM. I waited at the airport for more than two hours, and finally my "trainer" showed up. He had not been detained for any particular reason, he was just late.

We headed downtown to have a "working lunch." On the way to his favorite restaurant, he decided it might be a good idea to stop off at the local sporting goods store and check out some new fishing equipment. After an hour or so in the store checking out the latest fishing poles, we made our way to a rather unique luncheon facility where the waitresses seemed to be featured as much as the food. After lunch, my mentor suggested we take in a movie, which we did. As we concluded the afternoon training session, my guide said that he would not be able to spend any time with me tomorrow, since he was going to be very busy. He hoped I could get a cab back to the airport.

A day later, I arrived back in our Chicago showroom. My manager asked me what I thought of this top salesperson. Before I could say anything, my manager said, "He is one of the best. You're lucky that he spent time with you." To this day, I still do not know if this was a set up to put one over on the new kid or if my manager was really clueless. I did learn one important lesson: If you rely on other people to give you the information you need to succeed, you may be waiting a long time. If you really want to know how to do something, find out how to do it yourself.

I heard of an organization that claimed that when they send a new group of salespeople to an extensive training course, approximately 15 to 20 percent become successful. Over a period of time, because of budget restraints, the company reduced the training programs and still 15 to 20 percent of the new salespeople became successful. In recent years, they have almost totally abandoned the official training program, and yet to their surprise, 15 to 20 percent of their new hires turn out to be great salespeople. If people really want to be successful, they will find a way to do it, no matter who sets an example.

3

Get Connected

Everyone who works, interacts, or communicates with other people needs to understand how to get his or her message across. Understanding individual types of people and careful observation of the ways people act can make your interaction and communication more effective. It is just as important that you understand your audience as it is for them to understand you.

Become a Swan

Whether you are providing a service, hosting a client trip, or giving a presentation, never break out in a sweat.

We have a group at Herman Miller that arranges all of our corporate events. They do a wonderful job and every event appears to come off without a hitch. One day, I commented on their work and asked how they consistently accomplished their goals without any trouble. One of the managers said, "Well, it's because we're all swans." I asked what she meant by that. "Have you ever watched a swan swim along a shore?" she replied. "Have you noticed how effortlessly they seem to glide across the water? But if you look under the water, you would see that their little feet are going like crazy. That's what it means to be a swan." The next time you face some unexpected problems, your demonstration does not go as planned, or your client makes a last-minute change to the agenda, remember you, too, can be a swan. Make it look easy, even if your feet are moving like crazy.

Is Anyone Listening?

In life and in sales, it is important how you relate to your audience. Communication is unfortunately a dying art.

Once a coworker came into my office and started to go into great detail about some problems she was having with a client. As she spoke, I started to imagine what I thought were some awesome solutions. And so, before I could forget these pearls of wisdom, I interrupted with my advice. From my point of view, I was delivering timeless wisdom and interacting with her. Unfortunately, as far as she was concerned, I was only interrupting her presentation. Finally she said, "I don't want you to give me any advice. I just want you to listen. I know what I need to do. I just want to express it to someone."

From that day on, whenever I had a discussion with her, I would ask, "Am I just listening, or do you expect me to do something?" Maybe it's a guy thing, but if you are the type who always wants to solve the problem, make sure the person telling you the problem wants your solution. This is important to remember as a manager and as salespeople. Be careful that you do not just jump in and try to solve all the world's problems. As the old phase goes, "You're given two ears and one mouth. Use them in that ratio."

I have also found out that some people tend to nod during a discussion or presentation. This happens mostly with women. Although they may seem to agree with what you are saying, that may not be the case. We are sometimes lulled into a false confidence that our audience fully appreciates, understands, and agrees with everything we say, only to find out later that our listener selected another product or point of view. The act of nodding does not necessarily mean assent.

Another physical feature to consider when dealing with a one-to-one conversation is the pupil of the eye. If the person is interested in what you are saying, his or her pupils will begin to dilate. This is true unless, of course, your listeners are looking into the sun or other bright lights. If while you are talking the person's pupils do not dilate and he or she actually begins to look down or away, chances are that person is not really interested in whatever you are talking about. Change the subject!

Here is one last thing. Listen to *what* people are saying, but pay attention to *how* they are saying it. Listening to people's tones of voice will tell you more about them than their words will. Are they upbeat or defensive, cautious or spontaneous? A pause before an answer usually means a negative answer is on the way.

My father once said, "There is always seriousness to jest." Remember that when people are "kidding," they might just be sending you a no-kidding message.

I Think He Said...

Apparently, when the Continental was first shown to Lee Iacocca at Ford, he made a comment regarding the famous roofline. Lee reportedly asked, "What's with the porthole?" One of the designers assumed this was a negative remark, and the roofline was redesigned and the porthole was removed. Upon seeing the production model without the porthole, Lee asked, "What happened to the porthole?" The response from the designer was, "We understood you didn't like it, so we took it out." Lee is reported to have said, "No, I did like it. I thought it was really great." The porthole was back!

I am not sure if this is a true story or not, but it illustrates a good point. If you misunderstand a particular comment, sometimes you can waste a lot of time and energy. It is especially important, as a salesperson, to say exactly what you mean and to make sure people understand it in the way you presented it. Also, make sure you are hearing people as they want to be heard.

Keep Them Talking

George Smeenge has a commanding voice and piercing blue eyes. Sometimes George could say more with his eyes than he could with his mouth. If during a sales encounter someone would disagree with George or toss out a challenging question, he had the wherewithal and the self-confidence simply to look at that person. It wasn't in an "are you crazy" or condescending way, but in a way that actually made that person stop and rephrase the question, or in some cases answer the question for himself or herself. I learned from George that sometimes things *not* said can be even more beneficial than things being said.

We often like to monopolize the conversation. Many times, we are better off listening, looking, and letting clients come up with their own explanations. One thing to keep in mind when you are talking with someone is to ask open-ended questions, questions that cannot be answered by a simple yes or no. Open-ended questions invite more detailed answers. They allow other people to lead the conversation.

If you ask too many closed-ended questions, the person may feel like you are trying to interrogate him or her or playing a game of twenty questions. Sometimes, this results in more questions on your part and fewer answers on the person's part. Switch to open-ended questions fast! Sometimes a question like, "What would you do in that case?" leads to the answer, "I don't know." Then you can ask, "Well if you did know, what would you do?" It is amazing how the person, who only a second ago was clueless as to how to solve a problem, can now come up with a plan with a little help. When someone obtains a goal or is recognized for an accomplishment, try not to say, "You must feel good about that." He or she can only respond either "I feel good," or "I don't feel so good about that." Ask an open-ended question: "How do you feel about that?" or "How does that make you feel?" This will let people present their feelings as they see fit. Once this happens—let them talk! Let them enjoy the attention and glory on center stage. Do not jump in with a story of your own, even if you think it complements their story. This will come across as one-upmanship, or even competition.

Treat Them Like Clients

Have you ever noticed that good salespeople will go out of their way to please a client? They will accept rejection, apathy, and unreturned phone calls—and *still* accommodate their client's every need. Sometimes I think we should treat everybody like clients.

How Do I Fit into This?

Back in my college days, I worked for Herman Miller, Inc., during the summer break. One summer, I was a working in the factory where we were producing a new product called Action Office. I had no idea what this product was or the function of the particular part that I was making. My job was simply to snap small cloverleaf springs on a piece of extruded vinyl. After I had survived a week of this ho-hum-what-am-I-doing-here job, my supervisor walked up and asked if I knew what I was making. I replied that I had no idea. He took a few moments and walked me to his office, where he produced a brochure showing photos of this new product line. He then gave me a quick overview and pointed to one small item in the photo. It was the component that I was assembling, a trim piece used to finish off the end of a panel run. Then I realized what my contribution was, however small, regarding this product. I didn't necessarily enjoy my summer job any more than I had before, but I did know what part I played in the overall process, and that made a difference.

We often forget to tell people their role or contribution to a given activity. Think how much better we all work when we know where we fit in the overall scheme, when we know our position in the larger picture. Think of a jigsaw puzzle where the solution is shown on the box cover. Without knowing what the puzzle looks like when completed, it is really much more difficult to figure out where the individual pieces go.

This concept helps me deal with clients. It can be very difficult for clients to understand the different pieces of a presentation if they are not sure what the end product is supposed to look like. With all the technology we have at our disposal, we have the ability to deliver so much information that we bury our clients with it. We need to remember *not to add garbage to their plate*. We need to deliver our information in a manageable way. I took a speech class many years ago and heard somebody say that in a good speech you do the following three things: tell them what you are going to tell, tell them, and then tell them what you told them. If your client ever asks where are you going with this information, he or she is not seeing the total picture, and you are about to lose!

Use It, Don't Lose It

A few months ago, while driving to an appointment, I noticed that a fast-food restaurant that I frequently visited had closed. My first thought as I passed the empty building was that this was going to be a real inconvenience for me. This was one of my major fast-food stops. After a couple weeks of passing the closed restaurant, I noticed how it had already started to look old. In just a few more weeks, cracks appeared in the driveway. The windows were dirty. The sign was damaged, and the entire site was showing signs of deterioration and abandonment. It was hard to believe that only a short time earlier this was a busy drive-through restaurant.

No matter what, if you do not pay attention to maintenance, things deteriorate. I was thinking how true that is with so many things in life. Whether it is a skill, a relationship with a client, or your health. When was the last time you checked on the condition of your skills and client relationships?

AM or PM

In a recent conversation with some schoolteachers, I learned that many teachers tend to be morning people. They get up early to exercise, review their goals for the day, and drink their four cups of coffee, and they are ready to educate the world. On the other hand, many students tend to be evening people. Teenagers think it is a major accomplishment just to get up at the crack of noon. Some students tend to perform better later in the day and continue to rev up as the evening approaches. Think of the potential conflicts if the teacher is an AM person and the student is a PM person. And we wonder why the first-hour class can be the most difficult to teach.

We need to remember this when working with our clients. I try to be aware that people can be more or less receptive at different times of the day. Presenting to someone who is half-asleep or when you are too tired to be at your best simply does not work. Either they are not listening or you are not communicating. In any case, you are wasting their time and yours.

Too Close?

Salespeople love to be liked and enjoy other people. It is so much easier to do business with a friend, someone you know and can trust. But there is a danger in working with a close friend or possibly a relative. I heard it once said, "Never do business with anyone at whom you cannot afford to get mad." If this were a perfect world, there would never be any conflict in business or your personal life. Both parties would always win. The forecast would always be correct. The shipments would always be on time.

But this is not a perfect world, and sometimes the unexpected and the unacceptable happen. There are times when one must take an unpopular or undesirable approach to resolve a problem. Even though we try to be as diplomatic as possible, there is still an issue that has to be addressed. Dealing with these issues becomes much more difficult when you are dealing with a close friend. Remember to keep your business life and your personal life separate. Never sell your car to a relative. Never let a good friend manage your money.

Sales and Sitcoms

One of my hobbies is watching television. This is one thing I am very good at. Over the years, I have noticed that certain television shows seem to make it really big and others barely make it past the pilot. The sitcoms that make it seem to have the four personality types I heard described once in a training session put on by Wilson Learning in Minneapolis. The presenter said that there are four basic personality types found in today's population: the analyzer, the driver, the amiable, and the expressive.

The analyzer is constantly looking for more and more information. His or her biggest fear is making a decision without all of the available information and making a mistake. The driver feels that he or she must succeed at all costs. This person's biggest fear is failure. The amiable, the one who must be loved, is always the peacemaker and avoids conflict. He or she has an incredible fear of rejection. Last is the expressive, whose sole desire is to be comfortable at all times, who hates the thought of pain or having to work hard, and who tends to be a little off-the-wall. Naturally, he or she fears being uncomfortable.

In successful sitcoms like *Seinfeld*, *M*A*S*H*, or *Everybody Loves Raymond*, you can quickly recognize all four personalities. I think each one of us falls into one of those four categories. Now I know this is much simpler than many other schemes for describing personalities, but this four-way division helps me understand my personality and how to communicate with other kinds of people.

This means that only 25 percent of the population is like me. If I were an analytical type, to 75 percent of the population I would be a nitpicker. If I were a driver, to 75 percent of population I would be known as an SOB. If I were an amiable type, to 75 percent of the population I would be a wimp in need of acceptance. Since I am probably an expressive type, 75 percent of the population thinks I'm a little off-the-wall.

These different personalities can result in some difficult relationships. Take, for example, an expressive salesperson reporting to an analytical manager. The manager needs information and requests reports. Salespeople typically hate paperwork, see no reason to fill out forms, and may be late in providing the requested information. The manager thinks that the salesperson is defying his or her request. On the other hand, the expressive salesperson can't understand why this manager needs all this "worthless" paperwork.

Questions

The older I get, I find myself asking, "Why is it that people so seldom say thank you?" Do I make a point of thanking people for a specific gift or action? I'm trying. Have I taken the time to thank my clients for purchasing our products and services? I *really* push myself to do this. Have I thanked an employee for a job well done? Not often enough. Have I thanked my employer for his constant support? Ditto. Have I thanked a coworker for contributing to my success? Have I thanked my spouse for her patience? She certainly deserves it. Have I become so desensitized and careless that I just do not feel it is necessary to say thank you?

Mirror, Mirror on the Wall

So much of sales boils down to relationships. So much of *life* boils down to relationships. Working with people, understanding their needs, trying to solve their problems, and making them happy are all in a typical day's work for a salesperson. For the most part, working with people is an enjoyable and educational process. But once in a while, I will run into a person with a certain habit or mannerism that drives me up the wall.

I have come to realize that so often the characteristics or actions that irritate us most are the same characteristics and actions we ourselves have or take. The things that parents complain about in their children are the same characteristics they themselves are known for. We may find it is hard to work with a fellow salesperson because he or she is so competitive or controlling. Yet the reason this person frustrates us is because we *also* want to be in control. It is a good idea to practice a presentation in front of a very good friend willing to tell you exactly what worked and what did not. It's also a good idea to ask your good friend if a certain characteristic that drives you crazy might not in fact be something you have in ample supply.

4

Get Pumped

Now that you have a better understanding of your clients, your resources, and yourself, and you have honed your communication skills, it's showtime. The following proven suggestions, techniques, and recommendations will help you to do your best when you present an idea, a point of view, or a product. A presentation does not have to be nerve-racking, but it should always be exciting—you are much more convincing when your adrenaline is flowing.

Are They up for It?

A very important point about any sales call is making sure the client is in the right frame of mind. Just like you have to be prepared for your presentation, you also have to make sure that the client is prepared for your presentation.

Years ago in Minneapolis, I had the good fortune of working with a young lady named Ricki Arnold, who worked with Facility Systems, Inc., our Minneapolis dealer. We had been awarded the Minnesota State contract, and Ricki was meeting with the local school board, which was working on a new project. The meeting began in our dealership's showroom after 5:00 PM. As the school board members started to file into the conference room, it was obvious that they had all had a long and busy day. When Ricki began her welcome and to review the agenda, she noticed that most people were leaning back in their chairs with their arms crossed and with rather uninterested looks on their faces. It was almost like a challenge that said, "This better be worth my time."

Ricki just stopped. She looked at the school board members and said, "This is not working." At this, every eyebrow suddenly went up. Ricki took an entirely new direction. "You have an opportunity to create an environment for the students and faculty to study in and to work in day after day. So few people ever get a chance to really create anything during their lives. This should be considered a great challenge, a wonderful and rewarding opportunity, and yet you're looking at this right now as if it is the worst task you have ever been assigned."

It was amazing to watch the transformation. They all sat up and looked at one another. They uncrossed their arms, and their faces seemed to say, "This is important. We have been given the opportunity to create a very important learning environment, so let's make the most of it and have some fun doing it." The meeting continued. The audience was now ready, and Ricki gave a very successful presentation.

Sometimes you need to stop and take a chance. If Ricki had not challenged her audience, they would have sat through her presentation, left, and never really become part of the creative process. More importantly, Ricki might not have gotten the order.

Although I have never dared to challenge my audience the way Ricki did, I have incorporated her actions into many of my presentations. A great way to start off a presentation is to challenge an audience by reminding them that although most people never get the opportunity to create anything, they have the chance to create an environment where people are going to live and work for more than two thousand hours a year—that's more of their waking hours than they spend at home. This can become a powerful opening statement that will cause your audience to see the importance of your information and their participation.

You're the Message

Once you secure an appointment, you have prepared for the sales call, and you are in front of the client, "It's showtime!" There are many books written on how to give a fantastic presentation. However, one of the best lessons I learned came from a fellow salesperson.

When I was first introduced to presentation skills, I was running the AV booth for my company during our client seminars. AV, which stands for audio visual, is a term we hear today about as much as "8-track." Nobody under the age of forty understands it. Anyway, I had the opportunity to run the AV booth and observe different presenters.

One presenter, a dynamic speaker, taught me a great lesson. Back in the old days, we did not have PowerPoint. We had 35-mm slides, which basically did the same thing PowerPoint does today, only with a lot more things that could go wrong. This presenter, Con Boeve, had a wonderful way of relating to the audience. He always kept his eyes focused on them and they kept their eyes focused on him. This is because *he was the message*. The slides he used were simply background scenery. The slides were not the message. He also knew his presentation so well that he never turned to look at the screen. He was *always* fixed on the audience.

I asked him how he always knew where he was in his presentation, so that he never had to turn around. He said, "I just look at the glass in front of the projection room wall, and I can see the reflection of what's on the screen." This allowed him to concentrate on his audience. The same technique holds true for PowerPoint presentations today. If you have your laptop positioned so that you can glance at your computer while the Infocus projector is displaying your slides on the screen, you can keep your eyes on the audience.

Remember, *you* are the presentation, *not* the slides, *not* the PowerPoint. Today, we seem to be putting so many words, diagrams, and symbols on each slide that they read like a brochure. The audience is so busy trying to digest the information on the PowerPoint slide that they do not pay attention to the presenter. If the information on the screen is more important than the presenter, then why do we need presenters? Just hand out a copy of the presentation!

Never forget that you are the presentation and that your PowerPoint or slides are simply background scenery to make *you* look better. Make sure that the slides only support your message and are not a substitute for what you really want to say or want your audience to remember.

Showroom or Classroom?

Back in the early 1970s, Herman Miller introduced a new concept for office furniture called Action Office. This product was the beginning of the "open office," or as we know it today, thanks to Dilbert, cubicles. Because it was a new concept and people resist most new things, Herman Miller needed to find a novel way to bring this revolutionary product to market. With the inspiration of Joe Schwartz's creative genius, Herman Miller developed the Educational Center, a converted grocery store in a shopping center located in southwest Michigan. Potential clients would come there and invest two days to receive an education about offices and office work. They would hear nationally known speakers discuss office productivity and what can cause disruptions. How do people communicate? What role does your facility strategy play in your business strategy? What is the cost of change? It was as if the client had signed up for a college course on how to achieve office productivity.

The groups spent most of their time in the classroom. They left to tour the display area only after all of the office issues were discussed and solutions were presented. This was no sales pitch, but rather an educational seminar. Or maybe it was a sales pitch that did not look or sound like any other sales pitch in the world. I think that is why someone like me, with a degree in secondary education, was so attracted to Herman Miller.

Today, so many people want to give a moving sales pitch, but clients really want information that helps them perform their jobs. We need fewer showrooms and more Educational Centers. We should work less on giving sales pitches and more on hosting seminars.

I have heard it said that people do not change their minds once they arrive at a decision. However, one can arrive at a new decision based on additional information. Shouldn't a salesperson be providing that additional information? When was the last time you asked yourself what information would take your client to not only a new understanding of his or her job, but also how to do the job better?

It's Alive!

As a result of the Educational Center and our approach to educating clients, we became well-known for the successful introduction of the Action Office system. We were not as successful with our seating lines. In many competitive projects, we would be awarded the workstations, but the seating would go to a competitor.

In 1976, we introduced a new type of chair called Ergon. Ergon was short for ergonomics. It was the first chair on the market that dealt with the science of ergonomics. Because so few people understood this term, we would begin our presentations by explaining that ergonomics was the science of how one relates to his or her environment.

People found this very interesting. We were not just presenting this product as a comfortable chair, but rather as a component important to one's health. We talked about vascular and orthopedic issues. We talked about how people sit and how they move. We discussed how they change position in the chair from a work-intensive position to more of a conversation or reflective mode. We talked about pinch points and pressure points. We talked about the sacrum and the ever-important tailbone. Our presentations were designed to educate people about what happens to them when they are in a chair.

As in the Educational Center, we would spend most our time discussing the issues. Only after these discussions would we show or have the client sit in the Ergon chair. One day a competitor of mine was quite taken aback after losing a major seating bid to my new chair. The sales rep with the competitive company approached me and said, "This new chair of yours is really no different than any other chair on the market. The difference is you guys from Herman Miller can romance the daylights out of these things." With that, he proceeded to kick my chair across the room.

I have never forgotten that day, or his comments, because that's exactly what we did. We romanced the products. We made them come alive. The Ergon was not just a chair. It was something that gave people health. This chair was something to which people could relate. After they heard our educational presentation, they became seating experts themselves. Every time they sat on any chair or sofa, they could not help but wonder what was going on with their bodies. Were they getting proper seating support and sitting in the best posture?

I learned an excellent opening statement for a seating presentation from a gentleman in Bloomington, Illinois, by the name of Don Bollinger. Don was truly a seasoned, professional salesperson. Don would begin his presentation with the following attention-getting statement: "Seating is the most important piece of equipment that you're going to invest in for your organization, because it is the only piece of equipment that can give your employees personal comfort. Now I don't mean comfort in terms of falling asleep or sitting in a La-Z-Boy, but comfort from the fact that they can concentrate on their task, do their work, and not be uncomfortable or feel that they need to get up and take a walk because their back hurts."

This original opening for a seating presentation transformed the chair from simply another piece of furniture that needed decisions on color, style, and fabric to an important ergonomic evaluation. This product can affect the productivity of an organization. I have used Don's opener on every chair presentation I have ever made.

If I Say So Myself

My last chair presentation was so good, I stopped halfway through it and bought one myself! It doesn't hurt to impress yourself every once in a while.

Let Us Entertain You

People love to watch demonstrations. Back at the Educational Center, before letting them see the Action Office display, we would spend some time preparing visitors for just exactly what they were going to see. After presenting the concept behind the product, we would assemble a small 6x4-foot workstation in front of the audience. We took one component like a divider panel and pointed out its unique design. Then we would take out a connector and then another panel. While we were talking about it, we would actually build a workstation. We would complete it with a shelves, work surfaces, and bins for filing. No one had ever seen a workstation built before his or her very own eyes. And if that weren't enough, we would rearrange it. We might raise or lower the work surface to show how easily we could accommodate the height of a user. Or we might add an additional panel to make the workstation larger. People would be sitting on the edges of their seats watching our product demonstrations.

Audience response is nothing new. Have you ever had an opportunity to go a county fair and watch the people stand around the Vegematic display? Or watch people fixate on a person sharpening a knife and then slicing a piece of newspaper into ribbons? Now, of course, this happens on television all the time. People simply love to watch demonstrations.

People love to hear stories. People hate to be lectured. Can you take a feature or benefit of your product and turn it into a meaningful and interesting story? I guarantee you, it is better to go along with human nature than to try to change it or ignore it.

Then Again…

I was working with a young lady named Denise Sarles on how to give a dynamic chair presentation. We practiced it over and over in preparation for a presentation she had scheduled with a potential new client. On the day of the sales call, I was waiting to see her well-thought-out and practiced chair presentation. After a brief initial discussion with the clients regarding their needs, Denise simply produced the chair and said, "Sit on this one. You'll love it."

The people sat down and said, "This is great! Let's go with this one." I almost told them that they had to listen to our presentation before we would sell them the chair, but I didn't. Each person has his or her way of doing things, and what really matters is getting the job done. It also reminded me that experience isn't everything.

"Subtle Little Differences"

A dealer in Minneapolis gave me a phrase that I will always remember. He had a wonderful way of making a major point with a minor item. Because Herman Miller is not a low-cost provider, it is important for the client to see the quality that Herman Miller puts into all of our products. To demonstrate quality, the dealer would call attention to the connection between the metal shelf and the molded end panel of our shelving unit. He would take a screw out of the side panel of the shelf component and show the client that it was a machine screw. Not a wood screw. This machine screw attaches to a metal insert molded into the end panel of the shelf. This is a metal-to-metal connection. Not a wood screw into particleboard, as most of our competitors use. He would then point out that metal to metal can be tightened and loosened many times without wearing out. This is not true for wood screws and particleboard.

Then came his winning statement. "It is the subtle little differences that separate Herman Miller products from the rest." Once the client acquired this mindset and began to realize how much attention Herman Miller gave to a simple screw attachment, imagine how she viewed all of our other products from a hardware standpoint. Think about the new way she looked at our competitors' products.

Mine or Theirs?

When you hear people talking about their organizations or stating a philosophical or political belief, pay close attention to the words they use and you will get a good reading of their commitment. When somebody constantly refers to the organization that they work for as "them" or "they," you quickly realize that there is more than a little separation between the organization and that individual. When an individual uses the words "my" or "our," you see at once that the speaker is connected, supportive, and feels ownership of his or her company.

I once heard a speaker who was obviously very much a part of his organization. During his presentation, he used phrases such as "*my* company," "*we* deliver," "*our* commitment to you is," and "thank you for purchasing *our* products." Toward the end of his presentation, I asked the person next to me whether the speaker owned that company. He spoke with such conviction that I thought he must own the company—or at least be a major stockholder.

When you are speaking to an audience about your organization, your choice of words will have a major effect on how they view your relationship to your company. The stronger the bond you convey, the more credible, convincing, and believable your presentation will be. It is *your* company. You are its representative. You are speaking on its behalf. Take ownership and your audience will respect you for it.

Humor Is Serious Business

People love to laugh, and, if you have a great sense a humor, you are probably good at making other people laugh. But humor is a lot of work. Sometimes we think we are saying something clever or cute, but in reality we have said something that offended or distracted our audience. A number of people I have worked with have an incredible sense a humor and can say things that the average salesperson probably could not, or would not, say.

One such a person is Jerry Erickson. Jerry and I had been working with a major computer company in Minneapolis to outfit its assembly line. During the sales process, we had a mockup at our facility to demonstrate how our product would fit their manufacturing procedure. Thinking that the sales process was over, we sent our display product back to the factory. A week later, we got a call from the head of the manufacturing division. He wanted to stop by and review some of things we had talked about. A couple of his people were coming along.

A half-hour later, four cars drove up and sixteen people walked into our showroom. Jerry turned to the leader and asked how much time we had. The client replied, "We've got the rest of the day. I would like these individuals to experience everything I went through in your earlier presentation." Trying to be good swans, paddling like crazy under the surface, we glided into the conference room, sat them down, and put on an automated slide presentation of a rather simplistic corporate overview, which they, like the good Midwesterners they were, sat through politely. Looking at our watches, we realized we had used up five minutes of "the rest of the day." So we put on another automated slide presentation. This one dealt with design and color. Another five minutes went by. We showed a brief slide presentation that actually discussed some of the products they were interested in, but ten minutes later we were finished with that.

At this point, Jerry did the unbelievable. He stood up and leaned against the door leading out of the conference room. He turned to the manager of the group and said, "David, we're at a crucial point in the sales process. You can either sign the contract right now, or we've got a lot more slides back there," to which the client responded, "We'll sign, we'll sign, anything—just, please, no more slides." The entire room went up in laughter. We were able to go through some brochures, answer some questions regarding the product, and salvage the meeting. Jerry had the timing and the ability to use humor to defuse what could have been an embarrassing and nonproductive meeting.

Humor can also make a common item interesting. Herman Miller is known for its seating. Over the years, we have produced many revolutionary, trend-setting chairs. The casters on these chairs are not usually the feature that gets a lot of attention. There are a number of different types of casters available. Some are used for hard floors. Some are used for carpeted floors. Some lock. Some are over-sized to roll more smoothly on thicker carpets, and some have a very low profile. One of our presenters, while going through a rather in-depth presentation regarding seating, diligently explained all the different characteristics of the casters. This could have been a rather boring presentation, until he concluded by asking the audience to remember that all Herman Miller chairs are caster-rated.

Quick Thinking?

During a presentation to a major client, I demonstrated the ease with which our cubicles could be assembled. I was also in the process of explaining both the ergonomic and safety issues designed into the system. After I had finished building the workstation, I was ready to execute my favorite part of the presentation, which had become my signature act. My coup de grâce involved slamming the door of the top shelf down onto my hand.

When the door was closed, it covered all the contents on the shelf. When you wanted something off the shelf, you simply raised the door and rested it on the top of the shelf unit. The door was designed so that if I were to hold my hand on the front edge of the shelf, but off to the side, and slam the door down on my hand, it would not hurt. As soon as the door came in contact with my hand, the force was then directed to the other side of the shelf, which made a lot of noise but did not hurt my hand at all.

I was ready to complete my demonstration, knowing that I would get my normal, gasps of amazement from the audience. I had neglected, however, to attach the top portion of the door to the shelf. As I slammed the door down on my hand, the top portion disengaged, rose up, and smashed me right in the face. It literally knocked me to the ground. I am not sure just how long I laid there, but when I did look up, I saw people leaning over looking at me. My glasses had been knocked off, so things were a little blurry.

As I got back on my feet, I thought I'd better try to salvage the presentation somehow. So I looked at the audience and said, "Safety is really important to my company. If this had been anybody else's product, I would be dead." That was the last time I ever saw those clients. Always double-check your props.

Get In, Get Out

I have heard that one of the greatest fears people have is public speaking. In the life of a salesperson, giving presentations and talking to large groups is a major part of the job. Many salespeople, after years of giving the same presentation or working with a particular product line, feel they have the ability to wing it. In some cases, this is possible. Winging it for these people is not really winging it at all. They know what they are saying backward and forward.

Some presenters take the time to write out their entire presentation word for word. Many of these people tend to read the presentation. As a result, they seldom look at the audience for feedback. I always try to look at my audience as much as possible, rather than look at a script. To maintain eye contact, I memorize and deliver two things verbatim—my opening remarks and my closing comments. The opening needs to set the pace for the audience. It is their first impression of the speaker. They are looking at your mannerisms and are listening to the tone of your voice for enthusiasm and conviction. They are already asking questions about you. Are you going to be boring? Is this presentation going to be humorous? Will this presentation be educational? Investing time in creating a dynamic opener for any presentation pays real dividends.

The conclusion of a presentation is equally important. Too often great presentations drift off into soft-spoken, indistinguishable, rambling words, while the presenter picks up his or her notes and walks off the stage. Leave your audience with a positive impression! I try to make my endings recap my presentation and leave my audience with a challenging thought. And I always thank my audience for their attention.

The body of a presentation should consist of a number of key points. I try to leave myself the flexibility to move quickly past points that the audience may not be interested in and to be ready with additional information, or stories, to add to those points in which the audience does show interest. For every key point, I create a series of stories and subpoints to enhance the main points. When you see people lean forward, smile, and start really focusing on you, charge forward with those additional items you have tucked away in your back pocket.

The most important thing about a presentation is to know how to get into it and how to get out of it. If you lose your audience before you start, you have had it. And if you leave them with a whimper, they will not remember anything useful you have said. In with a bang, and out with a bang. That's my goal.

But Do They Like It?

Once you have become comfortable with your presentation, you run the risk of becoming bored with it. A lack of enthusiasm will come across to your audience; if you are bored with your presentation, you can be certain that your audience will also get bored with it. To keep this from happening, a fellow salesperson gave me this advice. Focus on a coworker or person in your audience who has sat through your presentation before. Speak directly to that coworker, and if you can keep his or her interest, you will definitely keep the interest of your audience. Find ways to refresh, enhance, or even rearrange your presentation to keep it new and exciting for someone who has seen it before.

Don't Refuse the Mint

One night on the way back home from our favorite pizza place, my daughter Karyn made an innocent suggestion. It may have had something to do with the garlic toast or the onion pepperoni pizza that we had just enjoyed. Whatever the motivation, Karyn said something like, "I'm going to have a mint, and I suggest that everyone else have one as well."

Sometimes in sales, it seems that everything is personal. At times in my career, people have told me something that could have been very helpful and yet I took it as a personal attack and refused to listen. Whenever somebody makes a negative comment about my presentation or my proposal, I try to maintain an open mind, but it is not easy. I keep telling myself that finding out what *doesn't* work, or identifying things that are *not* right, is just as important as finding things that *do* work, or validating things that *are* correct.

I remember a time when, after giving what I thought was an excellent presentation, a colleague took me aside and gave me a very critical review. It was certainly not what I wanted to hear. I was tempted to just turn him off like a bad radio station, thank him for his comments, and change the subject. My persistent colleague, however, was also gracious enough to point out that with certain minor changes, I could have a much better presentation. It took me a while to consider his comments rationally, but eventually I saw that, by taking his suggestions, I could improve my presentation and achieve the desired results. We all need to know what works and, more importantly, what doesn't work. We all need to stop every once in a while and see ourselves as others see us. So now, when someone offers me a mint, I lean back and enjoy it!

5

Get Smart

You may have done a great job of preparing for the adventure. You may have selected wonderful guides. You know how to communicate. You may have even given a great sales pitch, but there is more to success than just knowing your client's needs and executing an awesome presentation. You need to develop and exercise the necessary sales skills to complete the process, or you may not make it home to enjoy the rewards.

Change—Bad for the Incumbent

You have heard it said that, "You can't pick your family." It's also true that, "You can't pick your client's personnel." That is something outside your sphere of influence. In some markets, like Detroit, many of the facility or purchasing people have been in their positions for a long time. They have assembled a team of chosen suppliers. If you are working with them and helping to get the day-to-day garbage off their plates, they will continue to buy from you. If you are on the outside looking in, you will probably stay there.

In other cities, I have noticed that people with purchasing or facility experience tend to move from position to position or from company to company rather than stay in one job at one place for many years. When personnel changes happen, it can be a good thing if you are the one looking for the opportunity to gain entry to the account. It can be a bad thing if you are on the existing team with that account.

The reason is simple. People like to make a name for themselves. New people want to show that they can have a positive influence on their company, division, or group. No one gets ahead by standing still or maintaining the status quo. If you are on the outside, a staff change is a great time to introduce yourself to a new person and begin showing what you can do to make their life better and their organization more productive. Do some digging and find out where there's room for improvement. What did the current supplier fail to do for this customer? Develop a strategy that will fill this void, and demonstrate how you can add value to this relationship.

If you are the current supplier, a change of personnel can cause your world to become much more difficult. Have you become too relaxed and begun to take your client for granted? If so, now is the time to make up for your laziness. Imagine yourself as a competitor. What would be the weak points in the existing relationship? Then develop a plan to resolve these issues and build on the positive relationship you have with the client.

Ask yourself these questions:

- What would happen if my key contact at this client was replaced with someone new?
- How would I be perceived by this replacement?
- Have I become overconfident?
- Have I taken this client for granted?
- Have I worked to get the garbage off their plate?
- What do I need to do to protect my position?

Anyone Need the Restroom?

As part of my initial sales training, I often accompanied Ken Duthler on sales calls. One thing I remember, before we met with any client, Ken would always ask me if I needed to use the restroom. My dad would say the same thing just before we got into the car for a long trip. Ken had a really good point. The last thing you want during a sales call is a call from nature. The restroom stop became an image that reminded me to deal ahead of time with any issue that could cause a problem during our meeting.

My father, an auctioneer, had some similar advice: "If you are going to be in front of people, you'll need all of your energy and senses focused on them. You can't be worried about other things. If your hair is combed the way you like, your shirt is ironed the way you want, and the knot in your tie is just right—you have half of the battle won. Now, just focus on what you want to say."

So often we are tempted to go into a sales presentation unprepared. We may be running late or have too many things on our minds. When we notice we are wearing two different colored socks, suddenly we forget all about the substance of our presentation. We forget that we never get a second chance to make a first impression.

Before a sales call, make a checklist:

- Why would this client want to see me?
- What is my objective for this call?
- What materials do I need for this presentation?
- How will I know if this call was successful?
- What will be my next action step?
- What can I do to make my client's life better?

The Truth Is Good Enough

I worked with a Herman Miller distributor in Dubuque, Iowa, named Gus Pascual. Gus was calling on a client who had a uniquely shaped office space. This client was an existing customer and user of our office workstations. He had called the meeting to see if we could add additional cubicles to his space, since he was going to hire five more people. The space was already very crowded, and I was concerned that there would be no good way to add five more cubicles.

Gus asked the man to let him have the floor plan and give him a week to redesign the space with the new cubicles. Gus gave me a call a couple days later and said that he had finished a new plan. He asked if I would like to attend the next meeting with the client. I told him I would love to and asked him if he had managed to fit in five additional cubicles. Gus said, "Five people! I got fifteen more people in that space." I was amazed.

We met with the client, and Gus rolled out the floor plans. To the client's surprise and mine, not only were there the original eighteen workstations, but there were now a grand total of thirty-three workstations with room to spare. The client looked at Gus and asked, "Are you sure this is correct? Did you draw this to scale?" Gus answered, "Absolutely. I did the building in quarter-inch scale and the furniture in eighth-inch scale." The client said, "But, Gus, that won't work." Gus replied, "And neither will your building."

The client realized that he would have to build or acquire a larger space. And when he did, Gus got the order for the entire new office. Sometimes, you have to take a chance. (By the way, George Nelson said in 1956 that one of the principal beliefs at Herman Miller was, "The truth is good enough." It's still true.)

Earn the Right

In sales, probably the most difficult thing to achieve is scheduling the initial call. We have become a society that is always suspicious of solicitors. We are too busy to take phone calls. If we want something, we figure we can get it for ourselves. We do not like to be interrupted by people who want to schedule time with us, only to talk about things that do not interest us. Yet, for salespeople, the entire process begins by getting that first appointment.

I once worked with a very creative salesperson, Chuck Buth. Chuck was a master at getting appointments. There was an individual with whom we wanted to meet, but we were having a difficult time getting this person to schedule an appointment. During a phone conversation with this guy, he repeatedly said he was not interested in meeting with us. Chuck made a rather interesting comment. "I can understand that you might not have a need for us to meet now, but in the future, things will change, and then you might have a need for our products and services. When that happens, I don't want to be just another name on the street trying to get your attention." And here is where Chuck earned his money. "I want to have an opportunity to meet with you, understand your corporation, identify some of the issues that keep you awake at night, and prepare some things that my company can do for you. *I want to begin now to earn the right to do business with you in the future.*" Chuck got the appointment. After all, wouldn't you give some time to a person who is willing to earn your business?

And Keep Earning It!

If you take your client for granted and you do not continue to earn the right to do business with her, bad things happen. I think we can all recall situations in our lives where initially we were very impressed and happy to work with or acquire services from a particular group. But over time, we began to feel that they started to assume we would always be their client. They weren't as quick to respond to our needs as they once were. They were not introducing us to any new ideas. They acted like, "I have your business, and I don't have to go the extra mile." At that point, I think we all have the feeling that it is time to find somebody else to work with.

Remember there is a second part to Chuck's phrase: "earn the right to do business with you in the future." That is, we need *to continue to earn* the right to do business with our clients now.

Make a list of all the things that you are currently doing for your client. And then make a list of things that you are trying to provide to *new* clients. As you compare these lists, make sure that you are not shortchanging your existing account. If you are, you can believe that your competition is trying to earn the right to do business with your clients in the *very near* future.

Don't Wait Too Long

Let's say you have an appointment set for two o'clock. You get there in plenty of time to use the restroom. You look great. Your hair is perfect, and your socks match. You are ready to see your client, but you are told to wait. The client is not ready for you. So being the swan that you are, you wait and try to look busy by checking your voice mail. You wait, and wait, and you wait. You begin to ask yourself, "How long do I wait?" Maybe we need an exit strategy for sales calls.

A very successful salesperson once told me to remember that I am important to this client. They need my information. If they do not, why am I even here? Yet now, I think, there will not be time enough for my presentation. If I try to condense my thirty-minute presentation into only fifteen or twenty minutes, I will most likely be omitting some important information and doing my client a disservice.

Maybe it is time to do something many of us find difficult. After ten minutes, I could approach the receptionist and say, "Mr. or Ms. Client and I were scheduled for a half-hour meeting. Anything less would probably not let us cover what we need to cover. Would you please let Mr. or Ms. Client know that we should reschedule. I will call back tomorrow for a new appointment." This could be a dangerous thing to do, but in most cases, the client will respect you, understand, and reschedule. Ask yourself, "Would you do business with someone who has nothing better to do than sit in your waiting room all afternoon?" I ask to reschedule.

Touching the Bases

There are so many books written on the sales processes that it is hard at times to remember if you are doing everything you should. These books are good and sometimes help us focus on what needs to get done, how to prepare, and how to close a sale. But, sometimes, a simple illustration helps me most.

Ken Duthler, whom I've mentioned before, has a wonderful analogy for the sales process. Ken compares sales to a baseball game. To score a run, you must touch all of the bases. If you run from first to third without touching second, you might save some time, but you will be called out. And if you only get to third, it does not count as a run. Sales is like that. Generally, you will need to make contact with all of the key players in the account before you can make a sale. There simply are not any shortcuts.

Consider first base the "user group" of your product. You need to make sure that your product meets their needs and fits their budget. If they do not support your product, you might not get any further. Second base could be their facility group. They need to see that your products and services support their overall facility strategy and that they will benefit from working with you. Third base might be the purchasing group. They will need to see how your products compare to other suppliers' products, and that they are getting the most value for their money. And, finally, there is home plate, or top management. In many sales situations, they have the final say. You cannot score a run without getting past the catcher and touching home plate

If you leave out any one of these groups, you run the risk of not scoring a run. Somebody might not understand or agree with your presentation or your products and, therefore, throw your proposal out. There is usually some truth behind clichés like, "You need to touch all the bases."

Thank You

If you have the opportunity to pay someone a compliment, be specific. If I say "nice job," it sounds like an afterthought, a formality. I try to mention a specific detail. "I really liked the chart you put into your presentation showing the growth rate." It shows that I really appreciate the work and the information that went into it. It also shows that I am serious when I compliment someone. And I am.

For some reason, many of us are all too modest. We feel that we should shy away from or downplay compliments. Maybe they make us feel uncomfortable. If you are on the receiving end of a compliment, accept it! Remember that a compliment is a gift. Would you make light of, give back, or refuse a gift? Do not insult the giver. When someone gives you a compliment, say "Thank you. I appreciate that."

Strong relationships are made of such small things.

One Ring-a-Dingy

After 9/11, we cut back on our flying. We also cut back on our budgets because of the uncertain economy. Face-to-face relationships have not gotten any less important to salespeople or any less expensive or time-consuming. It takes time and money to go out and visit a client, but clients want to meet with and get to know the people with whom they are doing business. If you do not know it already, the world is fueled by relationships, not contracts.

Salespeople can learn a lot about clients by observing their offices. If you take a look around, you will get an insight as to who this person is and what the culture of their organization might be. Look for photos and awards, and ask yourself, "Is this person family oriented? Do they have pets? What are their hobbies? What groups do they belong to? Does this company have a specific image? What are they trying to convey to the public with their facilities? Are they people oriented?" The answers will be a great help to you in preparing presentations. You need to know your clients if you are going to add value to their lives.

It is true that you have only one chance to make a good first impression. It is also true that you are a stranger only once. After you meet face to face and develop a working relationship, much of your business can be done over the phone. This leads me to my next point. We all hate interruptions. We hate them so much that we have even passed laws to keep from getting those telemarketer calls during dinner. Phone calls sometimes cause great frustration and even lead us to angry reactions. Sometimes we answer the phone when we really should let the answering machine or voicemail take over.

Have you ever been in a meeting or at lunch with someone and their phone rings? To your amazement, they not only take the call, but also proceed to carry on a lengthy conversation in front of you. The person on the other end of the line must be more interesting and important.

When I phone someone, I try to remember to ask, "Is this a convenient time to talk?" Or, "Am I interrupting anything?" Most of the time, people will respond with a simple, "This is fine, go ahead." But in some cases, they ask if they can call me back. I am delighted to hear this response. It is a lot better than speaking to someone who does not have the time or mind-set to take my call right then. My question also shows that I respect their time. And I do. When I do talk to them later, it most likely will be a better conversation.

If you are trying to get rid of a caller who will not stop talking and who did not extend you the courtesy of asking if this was a good time to talk, here is a great way to disengage. When you finally get a chance to speak, hang up. No one will ever think that you hung up on yourself. They will probably assume that you were disconnected.

Words, Words, Words

Of the many training sessions I have attended, there is one I will always remember. During this session, the presenter said that every phrase can be either positively or negatively charged. He gave the following example. He asked which phrase would you rather hear, "I want to teach you something," or "I want to share some information with you." He made his point, and I understood immediately. The first example made me feel like I was an animal in need of discipline, and the second made me look forward to hearing what this new information might be.

Every time we speak, we need to choose each word carefully. What a difference a few words can make. How often have we heard someone start a sentence with "I need," or "I want," or the ever-popular, "You will"? Suddenly, we do not want to hear any more from this person.

When we address a client or a friend, we need to think about the words we are using. Add to that the inflection in our voice, and we realize how important it is to hone our communication skills constantly. A great way to practice is to give your presentation to a trusted friend—one who will tell you the truth. Ask her if there was anything that made her flinch or set her off on a tangent. Was there anything vague or irrelevant? Any inside jokes that might not make sense to everybody? And the most difficult question of all is, "Did I leave anything out?" Better to confuse, distract, or bore a friend than a potential client. I can always take my wife, Pat, or a good friend out for dinner as an apology, but I might not get a second chance with a client.

It's a Small, *Small* World

You may have heard the old phrase, "It's a small world, but I wouldn't want to paint it." In any industry, former clients can show up at different times throughout your career, even after they have changed organizations.

I know a salesman who was rather upset with a certain purchasing agent who worked for a major company that was looking for new office furnishings. The salesperson felt that this purchasing agent was undermining his position. So the salesperson did everything he could to discredit the purchasing person. A number of years later, a major organization, which was moving into this salesperson's territory, announced that a significant bid for furniture would be forthcoming. Shortly after this news "hit the streets," this salesperson got a phone call from someone with a very familiar voice. You guessed it. It was the same purchasing agent. He had moved to a new organization and had total responsibility for the major project. He had called the salesperson simply to inform him that in no way was he ever going to entertain a bid from him, let alone give him the business.

You never know when someone you have "crossed swords with" may suddenly show up as your client or have the responsibility for a new project you would like to win. Even when you are unsuccessful, remember to be a gracious loser. It's OK to meet with the client and find out why you were not successful, if your intention is to be a better contender in the future. However, don't take revenge or make personal attacks on your client. It may only come back to haunt you later.

This example is also true in dealing with your own organization. At times, every person finds himself or herself at odds with management. He or she may have an overwhelming desire to express in great detail his or her dissatisfaction. The next time this situation develops, and you are ready to tell them the way it is, remember the advice a good friend of mine gave me. He said, "Telling your boss off is a lot like peeing in your pants. It feels really good at the time, but the rest of the day you're just going to walk around damp."

May I Help (Take Advantage of) You?

Animals can sense fear. Customers can sense hunger. When a salesperson desperately needs to make a sale to pay his minimum-interest credit card payment, somehow a client knows right away. When a client senses that your only goal is to get an order, his or her perception of you as a resource greatly diminishes. Clients want to buy from salespeople who are helping them solve problems, not taking their money. When salespeople are successful, their demeanor persuades the client that the salesperson is working with them primarily to make the client's life better. The sale is a result, not a goal.

I've found that successful salespeople live their lives the same way as they pursue a sale: with focus, discipline, and persistency. Successful salespeople are also successful managers of their own finances. They do not run up credit card debt. They do not live beyond their means. Years ago, I heard some great financial advice—the 10-10-80 rule. This is *not* a new long-distance calling program. Divide up your take-home money as follows: take the first 10 percent and save it. Take the next 10 percent and use it in a charitable way. Take the remaining 80 percent and enjoy it. With a disciplined financial life, that overwhelming and harmful hunger to achieve that sale, at all costs, will not exist. Your clients will see a consultative, professional salesperson whose goal it is to make the client's life better, rather than an I-will-do-and-or-say-whatever-it-takes-to-get-your-money huckster. With a stable financial life, your confidence increases. You will close more sales. You will make more money. Don't forget: People tend to buy from salespeople who are in control of their own lives.

No News Is Bad News

You may have heard it said that no news is good news. But that is not true when you are waiting to hear about a project being awarded or when you have interviewed for a particular job. If people are not talking to you during those final days, there is a good chance that you will not be selected.

Spoken, Not Slurred

Have you ever listened to a long, detailed voicemail that concludes with the caller rattling off a telephone number so fast that you just cannot understand it? Why is it that the most important information, the telephone number, is the one piece of information that the caller neglected to state clearly?

I often ask the same question about introductions. Many times when we are introducing ourselves to people, we do not say our names slowly and clearly. Or when somebody else gives us their name, we are so busy thinking about what we are going to say that we do not even hear it. I saw a salesperson introduce himself by stating his first name, pausing, and then restating his first name again, this time including his last name. "Good afternoon, my name is John—John Doe." That sounds a lot like "James, James Bond," doesn't it?

When I hear a person's name for the first time, I repeat that name. If someone introduces himself to me and says, "My name is Bill." I reply by saying, "Hello, Bill. It's nice to meet you." Repeating a person's name will accomplish two things. First, it helps you remember the name. And second, people love to hear their name spoken.

When I have the opportunity to introduce someone, I try to follow a simple process. First, I tell the audience where the person is from. Second, I tell the audience something about the individual, their history, their accomplishments, and their current position. And third, I state their name. If I begin by saying the person's name, the audience may not be ready to hear it. After I build up to the name, the audience is ready to hear it.

This process is easier when you introduce yourself on the phone. When the person you are calling says hello, and you throw out your name, they will probably forget it because they never heard it. Try starting off with, "Hello, I am with the ABC Co., and I am responsible for your territory. My name is John, John Doe."

If We Own It, It Matters

Some things never change. I believe that people take greater pride, responsibility, and ownership for something that they have created, more so than for something they have been given. I have found that salespeople pay much closer attention to an account that they have created, rather than for one that they may have inherited.

Look at your accounts. You'll probably find that you maintain a much higher degree of concern and interest for the accounts that you created, the ones that you sold, than for the projects that someone gave you. That is human nature. To be a really great salesperson, you need to apply the same degree of ownership and pride to the accounts that you inherit as you do to the accounts that you create. You owe it to your customer, your company, and yourself.

Coins Come with Two Sides

During a heated discussion about a particular strategy for an account, I remember a friend of mine saying, "Regardless of how thin you slice it, there are always two sides." In every discussion, the person with an opposing view feels as committed to his or her view as you do to yours. So much of success in today's society depends on our ability to communicate and to work with other people. This is especially true in sales. One of my favorite techniques in preparing for a debate is first, take the position of my opposition, study as they would study, gather the information they would collect, and believe as they would believe. Then I develop my information in a way that would best counteract my opponent's beliefs, information, and research. "Looking at life from both sides," as the Judy Collins song goes, has helped me understand the people I'm working with and has also helped me become a better competitor in the battles for sales.

Who Ordered the Steak?

It is always important to identify the key decision-maker in an organization. A true decision-maker is probably the first person to arrive at the office in the morning and one of the last to leave at night. If you want to make contact with decision-makers, call them early or call them late. Chances are they will answer their phone.

Sometimes it is not always easy to spot the decision-maker, but you can look for certain things that help you identify the people who are *not* decision-makers. Here are some entirely instinctive and almost foolproof ways of finding who is *not* the decision-maker.

When you invite your clients out for lunch, take a mental note of who orders what. The person who orders the shrimp cocktail, baked potato, rib eye steak, and death-by-chocolate dessert is *not* the decision-maker. This person is simply taking advantage of a free lunch and time away from the office. The real decision-maker usually does not even have time for lunch and is not at your table. If he or she does go to lunch, that person tends to order a salad or something light.

I find that you can also learn a lot by observing a person's handwriting and his or her appearance. If the person tends to use a circle to dot the letter "I," this is usually a sign of someone with a fairly large ego, someone who loves attention. If that person also has monogrammed cuffs, you can *count* on them having one especially large ego. So if you are having lunch with somebody who orders a four-course meal, circles their "Is," and has monogrammed cuffs, you can feed that person's body and ego, but chances are you will not get any decisions out of him or her.

Sales, Poker, and Baseball

Being persistent is a necessary characteristic for a salesperson. You cannot make just one call and expect an order. You need to learn about the account, and you need to solve the client's problems—take garbage off their plate. You need to earn their business. This takes time. You also have to know when it is time to give up. Know when to hold them and when to fold them. If you are a high-quality producer and your client is obviously a low-bid buyer, you are probably wasting your time.

I try to imagine and keep in mind a client profile that will match my company's products and services to potential candidates for business. That helps, but we all have to deal with a little item called our ego. For some salespeople, ego is their downfall. Some salespeople believe that they can sell anything to any-body—and that is a useful attitude to have, as long as you know when to turn it off. Sometimes, we need to accept the fact that we are not going to make a sale and move on to other opportunities.

Maybe it is just easier to keep calling on somebody who is not going to buy from us. It is a form of playing office. You can send out lots and lots of letters and e-mails. You can make lots of phone calls. You can complain to your manage-ment about all of the rejection that you face. Outside of that, you really don't have to do much work. No follow-through, no real problem solving. Unfortu-nately, you really do not make any money either.

Successful salespeople focus their persistence and doggedness on the accounts that match their best client profile. Invest your time with potential clients, who truly see the products and services you provide as useful and are willing to pay the price that you ask. Never let your ego stand in the way of walking away from a nonresponsive client and finding new opportunities. If you are a true salesperson, you will never bat a thousand, not even with steroids. If you *are* batting a thou-sand, you are probably not making enough sales calls.

Matrix Management

I sometimes find myself reinventing the wheel when it comes to client calls. Yet I want to make every call as beneficial for my client as possible. I want to make every call effective and efficient as it relates to my time. My solution is to create five or six high-quality, informational modules that I can use as a point of discus-sion in face-to-face meetings or as a mailing. These modules cover a number of topics relating to the products and services that my company provides.

After identifying and developing these modules, I create a matrix. Along the left-hand side of the matrix, I list my key accounts. Along the top, I list the differ-ent modules of information. When I schedule a meeting with each account, I know that I have the appropriate information for each meeting. During the next few weeks I see each of my key accounts and present the first module. A few weeks later, I repeat the process with my second module. With five or six mod-ules, I have a way of meeting with my accounts consistently over many months and giving them new information. I am also strengthening my relationships with clients by calling on them with something useful.

What really makes this process interesting is that, while I am presenting a spe-cific module, a client will begin to ask questions or make comments that add to my information. By incorporating what I learn, I improve each module with almost every meeting. This process continues through the module's life.

Another way of using the matrix is to list the major steps of the sales process along the top. The first step might be as simple as identifying accounts. The second step might be calling on them and introducing yourself. The third step might be gathering information regarding their organization. Additional steps could include making product presentations, taking trips to existing installations, booking the order, coordinating the delivery and installation, carrying out follow-up activities, and writing the all-important thank-you letter and request for referral.

A matrix of accounts identifying the various steps of the sales process helps me quickly identify where I am in each account. If I reach an impasse in a particular account and I am not showing any progress on my matrix, I have a visual reminder to consult with coworkers and find another way of accomplishing the next step. By looking at the matrix, I quickly see my activity level. It is a simple tool that really helps me manage a lot of information on multiple accounts.

Sometimes, when I am especially brave, I also create a personal matrix. It becomes my conscience. Along the left side of the matrix are the days of the week. Along the top of the matrix are those particular activities and goals that I want to accomplish—personal time, educational time, exercise time, family time, spiritual times, self-study time, or community activities. Every day I check off my completed activities. Within a few weeks I quickly see where I have spent my time—and where I have not.

Show Them the Money

One of the most interesting and memorable sales meetings that I have ever attended included a presentation titled: "What does your client's work world look like?" To make his point, the presenter drew a stick person with the arms extended upward and the legs angled outward. Then around this stick person the presenter drew a box. The presenter said that the box represented the world of your client. "Imagine," said the presenter, "your client living in this box, but the box is not stable. It is constantly shrinking and closing in on him. The top of the box is constantly moving down, the bottom of the box is rising up, and the sides are beginning to move inward. Your client's job is to force the ceiling back up, keep the floor from rising, and to push back the encroaching walls."

He went on to say that the ceiling of the box represents inflation, which is eating away at your client's profit. The rising floor represents rising costs. Every day that the costs of material, manufacturing, and distribution rise, your client's world gets smaller. The walls represent his shrinking market share caused by encroaching competition, which is also constantly trying to lure away his best employees. This manager, your client, spends his days pushing back inflation, trying to hold down the rising costs, and pushing back competition, all while trying to keep his brightest and best employees.

Why is your client doing this? Simply put, the job of every individual working for any for-profit organization is to generate money. Whatever his or her role, that person's job can be measured based on increased revenue or reduced costs. Of course there are many ways to achieve this objective. This is where we salespeople come in. Our responsibility and the value we add helps our client make money. We need to ask ourselves, "How can we help hold back inflation, stop or reduce rising costs, or keep competition from squeezing our client out of his market?" Can we offer long-term contracts that guarantee fixed prices? Can we provide cost-saving suggestions by "value engineering" our solutions? Can we provide products that help attract and maintain the brightest and best employees for our customers? Remember, if we cannot help our customers obtain their goals of holding back inflation, reducing costs, and keeping the competition from taking away their people and markets, why would they even meet with us?

6

Get Going

Any adventure can be full of interesting lessons that can help you in your business and personal life. You just need to know how to recognize them. I strongly believe that everything happens for a reason, and every situation can be a valuable learning experience. The following experiences helped me to better understand my world. I hope they will help you to better understand yours.

Which Way to Run?

An old friend, Fred Warner, would ask great questions and he gave good advice. Once, when I was contemplating a job change within our industry, I solicited Fred's opinion. After explaining the new opportunity, I looked to Fred for his support. Fred asked me, "Are you running toward this new job, or away from your old one?" It really made me stop and think. It is a question that I now ask myself every time I contemplate making a major change. Am I running toward a new opportunity, or away from existing problems? If I really take the time to answer that question honestly, I have a better idea of my true motivation.

At our best, we tend to run toward new opportunities. If we see a change as something that will help us grow and develop, we should pursue it with all of our energy. However, if we're running away from something, we will never make it. Our past problems can always run faster than we can, and they will always catch up to us. We need to deal with existing problems by addressing them head on. Only when our past is resolved can we enjoy moving to the next challenge.

What's in Your Head?

At a workshop the instructor asked the audience, "Where do you get your best ideas? Working at your desk?" Suddenly there was a lot of snickering in the audience. Apparently, most people were thinking the same thing as I. We do not get our best ideas in the office. We get them in the shower, on the treadmill in the morning, or riding in the car. Sometimes, we actually get our best ideas while talking to somebody without fully paying attention to him or her. Some people even get their best ideas in church, where the mind can really wander. That's where Art Fry first had the idea for *3M's Post-it Notes*.

Do you have moments when you just cannot remember something, like a person's name or where you may have seen him or her before? And then later, when you are not even thinking about that person, his or her name suddenly pops into your head. Most people I know have had this experience. Let me tell you, as you get older it happens more often—that is, the forgetting, not necessarily the remembering.

Sometimes when I need to be creative or come up with a new presentation and I really concentrate, nothing seems to happen. The "old screen" just freezes up. Then, when I am doing something totally unrelated, I get what I think is a great idea. If I do not capture it, however, in just a few seconds it is gone. I try to write it down on paper or enter it into my Palm Pilot as soon as I can. One great way to record these ideas is to call my own phone and leave myself a message. I am always surprised the next time I go to retrieve my messages. I not only hear one from myself, but also realize I forgot that I had sent the message in the first place! Wherever you get your best ideas, go there as often as you can. Make sure you have a way to record your inspirations.

If You Couldn't Fail

One question has always inspired me: "What would you do if you knew you couldn't fail?" Many of us have great ideas about what we would like to achieve. But there is always the nagging doubt that we might fail, and, because we don't want to risk failure, we stick to the status quo. Think of the people you know who were willing to take a chance. More have succeeded than have failed.

Think how different our lives would be if we lived with the attitude that we could not fail. What would you do differently? From a sales perspective, what would you do to gain more business if you knew you could not fail? Have you ever thought about asking your clients what would *they* do in their organization if they knew they couldn't fail? What changes would they like to see take place? Maybe that is the beginning of a discussion about how you could provide them support and help them to achieve their goals.

Confident Enough to Share

A famous quote made by Charles Eames had to do with imitations of his designs. Charles designed the classic Eames Lounge Chair. At one time, there were many copies of the chair available on the market. Someone asked if it bothered him that people kept copying his chair. Charles's answer went something like this: "No, I'm not upset that they keep trying to copy my chair. I just wish somebody would improve on it." What a classic answer! So often we are afraid of people stealing our ideas. We should have enough confidence in our creations that, like Charles Eames, we too would wish that others would improve on them.

Push the Right Button

In the early 1980s, I had taken a position with our corporate office and was living in Grand Rapids, Michigan. One night about ten o'clock the phone rang. It was a good friend whom I had not seen for quite some time. He was in town for meeting. He asked if I wanted to join him at his hotel for a drink. I said that I would be right over. My wife asked who was calling so late at night. I told her it was my old friend Kirby Turner, that he was in town staying at the Hilton, and that I was going to run over and join him for quick drink. I assured her that it would not be a late night. "I'll be home within an hour," I proclaimed.

It was a snowy January night. I jumped in the old Mercedes diesel and drove to the hotel. Kirby and I go way back, and we had worked together for a number of years. We had a lot to talk about, since we hadn't seen each other for quite a while. After a couple of drinks, we were notified that the bar was closing. So like any old buddies would do, we ordered a few more drinks and had them sent to his room. There we sat and talked and talked, until, finally, I realized that it was three o'clock in the morning. This was not a good thing. Pat was sure to make some comment on my commitment to be home within an hour.

As I drove home in what had turned into a blizzard, I began thinking how I could sneak into the house and not wake anyone. To complicate matters, we had a rather long driveway, and the diesel would make a lot of noise. As I approached the driveway, I opened the garage door with the remote, lined the car up with the garage door, accelerated, and then killed the engine so that I could coast in. Mission accomplished! I was in the garage, and I did not think anybody heard me come up the drive.

The snow was blowing into the garage as I reached up and pushed the button to close the garage door. To my surprise, the garage door would not go down. I pushed the button again and again, four or five times. Then I realized why the garage door was not going down. I had been pushing the doorbell button. One gentle press on the *garage* door button, and the door closed perfectly. When I opened the house door, I saw Pat standing at the base of the stairs comforting our two daughters, and holding back our golden retriever. I remember her saying to the girls, "It's OK, it's just Daddy." The reason I tell this story is simply to leave you with a reminder: if you think you are doing the right thing and nothing is happening, make sure you are pressing the right button.

(By the way, the very next day I separated the buttons by three feet.)

Make Way!

Last spring, as I looked out our dining room window, I noticed a large mature tree with a lot of outstretched branches. Not too far away, a sapling had taken root and had grown straight up to within a few inches of the lowest outstretched branch of the larger tree. Over the next few weeks, the sapling appeared to stop growing. It remained at the same height until a windstorm broke off the branch that hovered over the young tree. Within days, the young maple shot up, and continued to grow until it came within inches of another outstretched branch of the larger tree. It was as if the mature tree was controlling the growth of the sapling.

So often we can unconsciously overshadow others and stunt their growth. Whether in companies or families, we need to provide sufficient space for people to grow. We also need space for our growth. What branch is hanging over you? What is keeping you from growing? Are you hanging over someone else? Are you willing to give them the space they need to grow?

Take Five

My mother-in-law is famous for taking a fifteen-minute afternoon nap. When my wife first told me about her mother's habit and how rested her mother was after such a short time, I was skeptical. But many people, Winston Churchill in particular, have discovered how right my mother-in-law is. In fact, the beautiful Charles Eames' Chaise was designed precisely for such a nap.

I like to take mental minivacations. During the course of almost any day, with all of its demands, stress, and schedules, I really benefit from a minivacation. I take these vacations by looking at photographs of great times or peaceful places, or by creating similar pictures in my mind. Maybe it is an image of me standing at the seashore with my golden retriever. Maybe it's a waterfall in Northern Michigan. Or maybe it is remembering how wonderful it was lying on the deck of a cruise ship, staring up at the smokestack, watching the white smoke gently drift off to the dark blue horizon. If just for a few moments, consider those places that give you comfort, peace, and relaxation. It is a great way to get refreshed.

The "Red Lobby"

Have you ever noticed that whenever you ask people to critique your work or to review something you have done, they tend to concentrate on the negatives rather than the positives? It is as though they think they have not done a good job unless they can point out some deficiencies. It is true that criticism can be constructive and getting input from people you trust is beneficial. But sometimes it seems that people just want to find the negatives.

There is a phrase in the world of interior design called the "red lobby." When a designer is working on a floor plan or creating a building design, he or she instinctively knows that clients will search and search until they can find something to reject or challenge. So why not make it easy for them? For example, a designer might intentionally use a color scheme, like bright red in a lobby, that he or she knows the client will find unacceptable. Consequently, the client immediately finds the item that he or she doesn't like and expresses his or her concern. The designer agrees, makes the necessary changes, and the client goes forward with the rest of the proposal finding it to be quite acceptable.

If you deal with people who tend to look for something to reject or criticize, why not give them something that is obvious, controllable, and easily changeable? They will be happy that they were able to give constructive criticism, and they will probably be more receptive to the rest of your proposal. Also, remember the next time you spot something that is not quite right in a proposal, it just might be a red lobby.

Find a Little Good in Every Disaster

We have been living in the same house for about sixteen years. It is a great house in a wonderful location. The family room, however, which was built on a slab and faces north, has always been cold. Even though the room had a wood-burning fireplace, we seldom used it because of the work involved in carrying in the wood, tending to the fire, and cleaning up the ashes. Just as the holidays approached, we decided it was time to get a gas log installed. So with great expectations, my wife and I visited a distributor for gas logs, made our selection, and even opted for the remote control.

After signing the paperwork and taking our deposit, the salesperson informed us, since this was a very busy time of the year, our installation might not take place until after Thanksgiving. I thought, "Well, no big deal, as long as we get it installed before Christmas and New Year's."

After Thanksgiving, I called to get an update. The salesperson said she would have to call me back. But I never got a call back. After a few more calls, I spoke with someone who said he would have to check on the schedule after speaking with the installer. After two more weeks of calling, the installer informed me that they had just ordered my log, and that it should be in next week. The phone calls continued through Christmas and New Year's. Every time I thought about that log or called about the situation, I got the runaround. I just got more and more upset. I had selected their business. I had not quibbled about the price, and I had even given them a 50 percent down payment. Yet, they would not return my phone calls or give me any indication as to when the log would actually be installed. In mid-January, I was still looking at a cold, empty fireplace. I had had it! After a few carefully crafted words to the owner, I got my deposit back.

The next day I went to another supplier. Within one week he installed the perfect gas log for less money. As I thought about how uncomfortable and angry the first dealer made me, I tried to look for something beneficial here. Then it dawned on me: I was a dissatisfied client! I felt taken advantage of and abandoned. How many times have I caused a client to have that feeling? How many times have I not returned a phone call or given a client the wrong information, or simply tiptoed around the truth?

The next time you are engaged in any type of purchase or require a particular service and it goes south, rather than get upset, think about what a great learning experience you just encountered.

Linda's Secret

Back in college, Linda always got great grades and yet never seemed to study. One day I asked Linda, "How do you remember all the things you need to get good grades?" She never took notes. She never read. She just went to class. Linda asked me, "When you hear a really good, juicy piece of gossip, do you remember it? Most people remember it in great detail. The trick to remembering any information is to convince yourself that everything you hear is gossip."

The next time you're in a meeting and you don't feel like taking notes, just pretend that the topic is some really juicy, sensitive piece of information that you can't wait to share.

Cookie Power

Back in the mid-1980s, my family lived just outside Minneapolis. Our two daughters were eight and six years old. It gets pretty cold in Minnesota from about late August to early June, so as a family, we spent a lot of time in our house. One Sunday afternoon, our two daughters were playing upstairs and my wife and I were sitting in the family room by the fire. My wife, Pat, was reading, and I was watching something on TV. Suddenly, stomping into this peaceful family room came my older daughter, Kathy. She complained that her younger sister, Karyn, had taken one of her toys and would not give it back.

This had been a rather busy week for me, and I was looking for some peace and quiet. I started to get out of my easy chair to put an end to this yelling, complaining, and screaming. Before I could say a word, Pat, without even looking up, asked, "Do you want a cookie?" Kathy stopped her tirade, and with a slight smile on her face, she asked if Karyn could also have a cookie. The next thing I remember was Kathy yelling to her sister, "Hey, Karyn, we can have cookies!" The house fell silent. Still in the process of getting out of my chair, I stopped and with total amazement looked at my wife. She had restored peace without even having to look up from her book. I asked her, "How did you do that?" She said, "It's really quite simple. Just take their minds off whatever they are complaining about, and get them to think about something else." Sometimes when I find myself in heated negotiations, I reach for the package of cookies I keep nearby.

Giddyup!

In an old George Carlin skit, he refers to business ethics as an oxymoron. However, I am proud to say that I have had the privilege of working with many people who are extremely ethical in their business practices.

I have thought often of the story that someone told me when I was a little boy. The English court was looking for a new driver for the horse-drawn carriage of the queen. Many people interviewed for this rather prestigious job. One of the questions asked of the candidates was this. "There is a very narrow stretch of road that the queen will use quite often. On one side of the road is a wall, and on the outer edge is a cliff. How close to the outer edge of a road could you safely drive the carriage without endangering the life of the queen?"

Some of the candidates claimed that they could drive the carriage within one foot of the edge and not endanger the queen. Another said that he could drive the carriage within a few inches of the cliff and not endanger the queen. The candidate who won the position answered, "I am not sure how close to the edge I can safely drive the carriage, so I will go as far to the other side of the road as possible."

You may think that this would make a cute little Sunday school story, and it was. The lesson was when temptation appears, run the other way. I know now that it is also a great reminder to each one of us to not risk seeing how close we can come to the edge in our business and personal decisions.

Check Please

Many times I have gone to a wonderful restaurant, where I was properly greeted, immediately seated, and addressed by the wait staff in a most professional and friendly manner. My order was taken and wonderful food was quickly served. The entire dining experience was a delight. But then, when I was ready to leave, I realized that I had not received my check. I began to look for my waiter. After a few moments of not spotting him, I concluded that maybe he had left to eat his own dinner. As the moments passed by, the positive elements of the dining experience began to disappear. From feeling like an honored guest, I had turned into feeling like my waiter's prisoner. Suddenly, the memory of the initial service and the quality of food faded. I started to recalculate the tip.

This experience relates to so many situations in the sales process. We can do everything right, but fall short in completing the last step. Unfortunately the client notices. If we forget the importance of the last step, every positive action prior to this step begins to fade. All of our work for perhaps months—or even years—begins to evaporate. And more importantly, our client begins to question our professionalism and capabilities. The next time you are out for dinner and you find yourself waiting for the check, make it a learning experience. Think how you make your clients feel when the last step of the sales process is not completed as they anticipated.

Half Is Empty

It is probably just human nature to try to do as little as possible and still get by. However, to excel in your career, you need to work toward higher standards. Many of our standards are self-imposed. We choose and strive to achieve that which is important to us.

I was raised in Michigan where the winters are cold. We all learned that an empty gas tank is a prime candidate for condensation, resulting in a possible frozen gas line. It is always easy to let the gas tank go down to a quarter, or an eighth, or even a sixteenth, before refilling, and we just hope that our gas line does not freeze. My father taught me early in life that "half is empty." When the gas tank falls to the half-full mark, it is time to fill it up. Over my driving career, I may have made more stops at a gas station than necessary, but I have never run out of gas or worried about the gas line freezing.

We can try to get by with as little as possible, let our gas gauges get close to empty, and become candidates for all kinds of problems. Or we can take a little bit more time, be more prepared, and eliminate most of the problems, while expending only a little more effort. It is important to keep your eye on your client gauge and make sure that your relationships do not freeze up.

Sure, I've Got Time

Have you ever noticed that the only time it is really fun to do nothing is when you're *supposed* to be doing something else that you really do not want to do? On the other hand, if you have nothing to do, then doing nothing is really boring. In college, when I needed to prepare a report or study for a test, I could find all kinds of minor activities to fill my time. Suddenly, it became very important for me to organize my room or to call home to see what my family was doing. It was also the time my shoes would get polished.

Some things never change. Every day people set key objectives and compile a must-do list. Like people playing office, they let too many unnecessary activities creep into their schedule. Somehow, these new activities shoot up on the priority list, crowding out the things that they really need to accomplish.

Wilderness Training

One day, after he saw an Egyptian beating an Israelite, Moses took it upon himself to punish the Egyptian and, in the process, he killed him. To escape with his life, Moses fled into the desert, where for many years he took on the lowly task of being a shepherd.

I can only imagine what went through Moses's mind. Here he was, one of the most powerful men in one of the greatest nations of the world, Egypt. Then, in just one day, with one act of retaliation, he was reduced to being a lonely shepherd in a dusty, dreary, desolate desert, living in fear for his life. The preacher from whom I heard this story observed that during the time Moses spent in the desert, he learned important desert survival techniques. This newly acquired knowledge would become most helpful to Moses when, in just a short time, he would lead the Israelites out of Egypt and direct them as they wandered through that same familiar desert.

I have thought about this story many times when reflecting on my own experiences. Whether perceived as good or bad at the time, all my experiences have been learning experiences.

Final Thoughts

So what is the message behind this book? Is it about sales? Yes, but more importantly, it is about learning. Someone once said, "When you cease to learn, you cease to live." I work hard to never let a day or situation go by without trying to learn something from it. Watch a swan glide across the lake, a tree grow, a fantastic presentation incorporate great graphics, or a fast-food restaurant deteriorate after it closes. Listen to the people you encounter. Every day, look for the one lesson that can make a difference in your life. Experience is a most wonderful teaching tool.

978-0-595-37542-4
0-595-37542-1

www.ingramcontent.com/pod-product-compliance
Lightning Source LLC
Chambersburg PA
CBHW021016180526
45163CB00005B/1977